D0205897

SLAVERY IN THE ROMAN WORLD

Rome was a slave society. Beyond the thousands of slaves who worked and lived in the heartland of the Roman empire, slavery fundamentally shaped Roman society and culture. In this book, Sandra R. Joshel offers a comprehensive overview of Roman slavery. Using a variety of sources, including literature, law, and material culture, she examines the legal condition of Roman slaves, traces the stages of the sale of slaves, analyzes the relations between slaves and slaveholders, and details the social and family lives of slaves. Richly illustrated with images of slaves, captives, and the material conditions of slaves, this book also considers food, clothing, and housing of slaves, thereby locating slaves in their physical surroundings – the cook in the kitchen, the maid in her owner's bedroom, the smith in a workshop, and the farm laborer in a vineyard. Based on rigorous scholarship, *Slavery in the Roman World* serves as a lively, accessible account to introductory-level students of the ancient Mediterranean world.

Sandra R. Joshel is professor of history at the University of Washington in Seattle. A scholar of Roman slavery, women, and gender, she is the author of *Work, Identity and Legal Status at Rome: A Study of the Occupational Inscriptions* and editor (with Sheila Murnaghan) of *Women and Slaves in Greco-Roman Culture: Differential Equations* and (with Margaret Malamud and Donald T. McGuire) *Imperial Projections: Ancient Rome in Modern Popular Culture.*

CAMBRIDGE INTRODUCTION TO
ROMAN CIVILIZATION

Cambridge Introduction to Roman Civilization is a program of books designed for use by students who have no prior knowledge of or familiarity with Roman antiquity. Books in this series focus on key topics, such as slavery, warfare, and women. They are intended to serve as a first point of reference for students who will then be equipped to seek more specialized scholarly and critical studies. Texts in these volumes are written in clear, jargon-free language and will integrate primary texts into a synthesis that reflects the most up-to-date research. All volumes in the series will be closely linked to readings and topics presented in the Cambridge Latin Course.

ALSO IN THE SERIES

Roman Religion by Valerie M. Warrior
Roman Women by Eve D'Ambra
Roman Warfare by Jonathan P. Roth

SLAVERY IN THE ROMAN WORLD

SANDRA R. JOSHEL

University of Washington

CAMBRIDGE
UNIVERSITY PRESS

CAMBRIDGE UNIVERSITY PRESS
Cambridge, New York, Melbourne, Madrid, Cape Town, Singapore,
São Paulo, Delhi, Dubai, Tokyo, Mexico City

Cambridge University Press
32 Avenue of the Americas, New York, NY 10013-2473, USA

www.cambridge.org
Information on this title: www.cambridge.org/9780521535014

First published 2010

Printed in China by Everbest

A catalog record for this publication is available from the British Library.

Library of Congress Cataloging in Publication data
Joshel, Sandra R. (Sandra Rae), 1947–
Slavery in the Roman world / Sandra R. Joshel.
p.   cm. – (Cambridge introduction to Roman civilization)
Includes bibliographical references and index.
ISBN 978-0-521-82774-4
1. Slavery – Rome – History.   2. Slavery – Rome – Social conditions.
3. Civilization, Classical.   I. Title.   II. Series.
HT863.J67 2010
306.3′620945632–dc22   2009040102

ISBN 978-0-521-82774-4 Hardback
ISBN 978-0-521-53501-4 Paperback

To Robert H. Joshel and Laura J. Joshel

CONTENTS

MAPS, TABLES, AND FIGURES

ACKNOWLEDGMENTS

This book relies on the fine work of many scholars and historians of slavery and the Roman world. As an introduction to slavery at Rome, it attempts to bring this scholarship to students and nonacademic readers without diving deeply into its technicalities or detailing its complex debates. However, all readers should be aware that where slaves and their owners are the topic, debates and arguments follow. My own focus on both sides of the relationship that lies at the heart of slavery, slave and slaveholder, will be evident in the pages that follow; so, too, my interest in how we understand and represent the position occupied by slaves, whose voices in our sources do not speak as loudly as their owners'. This emphasis means that my greatest debt in the field is to Keith Bradley, whose many articles and books have shaped our understanding of Roman slavery and debates about it.

The help of many people was essential to the writing of this book. Above all, I must thank Stephanie Camp, my former colleague in American slavery, currently at Rice University. She offered astute criticism on several versions of the book, helped me to think about what I wanted to say, and shared her own deep knowledge of slavery with me. I have learned more than I can say about Roman material culture from John Clark, Lauren Hackworth Petersen, and Margaret Laird. John Clark read the book with care and offered advice about images. His own work, especially *Art in the Lives of Ordinary Romans,* lays the ground for several discussions here. Lauren Petersen was always ready with suggestions about images and was sage about their interpretation. Margaret

Laird read several chapters, corrected errors, and offered insight into the life of Roman objects and spaces. As always, I am indebted to Amy Richlin for her critical reading of my words and for conversations about things Roman. This time around the latter focused on Plautus. Other friends and colleagues offered their advice on the book or individual chapters. I am grateful for the insights and comments of Tani Barlow, Alain Gowing, Carlin Barton, Lynn Thomas, and Sarah Stein. Several scholars generously shared illustrations from their own work, and I am very grateful to each of them named in the captions. Special thanks are owed to Michael Larvey for his beautiful photographs. Finally, I would like to express appreciation to Beatrice Rehl for the opportunity to write this book, her advice, and her patience.

This book is dedicated to my brother, Robert H. Joshel, and my sister, Laura J. Joshel, in love and gratitude for their friendship and strength.

CHAPTER 1

AN INTRODUCTION
TO ROMAN SLAVERY

Trafficking in persons is modern-day slavery, involving victims who are forced, defrauded or coerced into labor or sexual exploitation. Annually, about 600,000 to 800,000 people – mostly women and children – are trafficked across national borders which does not count millions trafficked within their own countries. ... People are snared into trafficking by many means. In some cases, physical force is used. In other cases, false promises are made regarding job opportunities or marriages in foreign countries to entrap victims. ... Human trafficking has a devastating impact on individual victims, who often suffer physical and emotional abuse, rape, threats against self and family, passport theft, and even death. But the impact of human trafficking goes beyond individual victims; it undermines the safety and security of all nations it touches. (United States Bureau of Public Affairs, Washington, DC, May 24, 2004)

The primary distinction in the law of persons is this, that all men are either free or slaves. Next, free men are either *ingenui* (freeborn) or *libertini* (freedmen). *Ingenui* are those born free, *libertini* those manumitted from lawful slavery. (Gaius, *Institutes* 1.9–11, trans. F. de Zulueta, second century CE)

On May 24, 2004, the Bureau of Public Affairs of the United States Department of State released a report entitled "The Facts about Human Trafficking." The facts include a firm assertion that slavery hurts the men, women, and children who are enslaved and "the safety and security of all nations it touches." Slavery is labeled a "crime," the slaves "victims," and those who enslave others "criminals." By

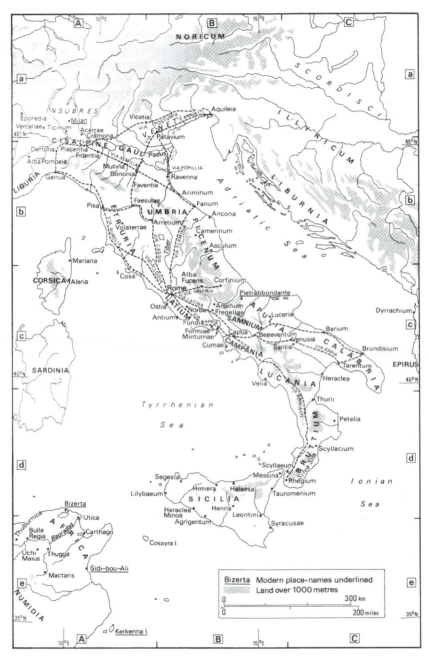

Map 1. Roman Italy. (From J. A. Crook, A. Lintott, E. Rawson, eds. *The Cambridge Ancient History*, Vol. IX, 2nd ed., Cambridge, 1994, map 2, p. 42)

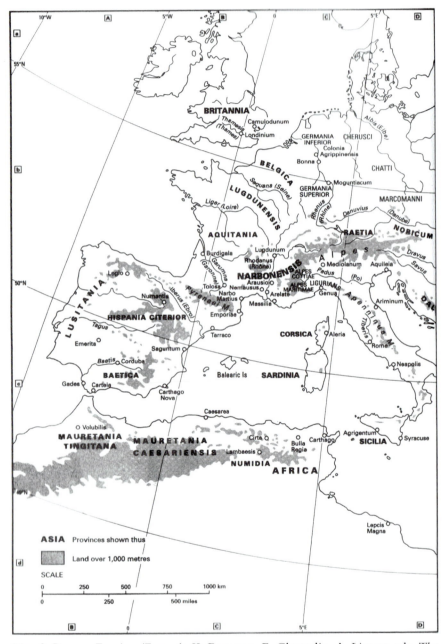

Map 2. Roman Empire. (From A. K. Bowman, E. Champlin, A. Lintott, eds. *The Cambridge Ancient History,* Vol. X, 2nd ed., Cambridge, 1996, map 1, pp. xvi–xvii)

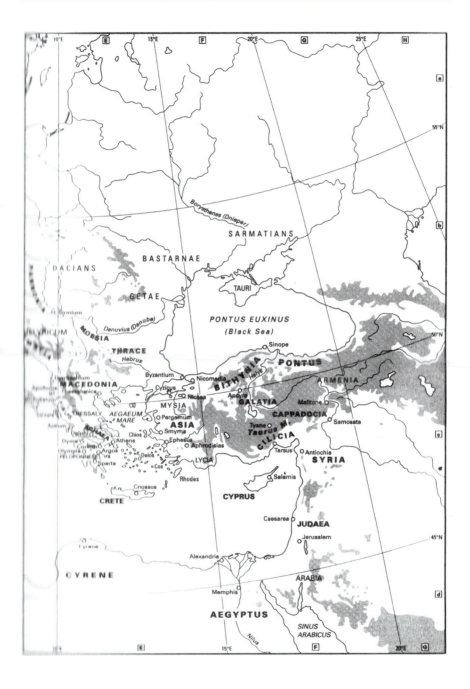

contrast, the ancient Roman jurist Gaius assumes that slavery is a part of Roman law. For the Roman lawyer, slavery is not a crime, and the enslaved are not victims; rather, as Gaius and other Roman jurists make clear, slavery, although not "natural," is a part of the law of nations. Natural law applies to all animals, not only human beings, but it concerns little more than the union of male and female, procreation of children, and their rearing. Everything that has to do with human culture and society – the state, property, commerce, and war – is covered by the law of nations. All peoples have their own laws, but the law of nations, including slavery, is common to all. In our terms, everybody does it: all nations have slaves, and there is nothing remarkable about slavery.

In North America and Europe today, we acknowledge that although there may be slaves in our world, we do not live in a slave society. We assume that slavery must be stamped out, that slaves must be freed. People who are sold in the early twenty-first century live in a world where there is an outside to slavery – although it is easier for us to know this than it is for a child sold to a brothel. Similarly, for slaves in the nineteenth-century American South, there was a free North and a public movement, abolitionism, that campaigned against slavery, calling it a wrong. Moreover, the Atlantic trade in African people was abolished in the United States in 1808 and in England in 1807, and, in the latter, slavery itself was abolished in 1833. For slaves living in the Roman world, there was no outside – no place without slavery and no movement that declared slavery wrong. Slavery was a normal part of life, and this was true not only for the Romans but for every neighboring ancient culture.

This ancient world and the men, women, and children living within it, both free and slave, are the subject of *Slavery in the Roman World*. The book has three goals. The first is obvious: to teach something about Roman slavery and the lives of Roman slaves to those unfamiliar with the topic. The second reaches beyond slavery itself: to understand Roman history and society, for slavery, its history, and its terms shaped every part of Roman culture. Last, I hope that thinking about Roman slavery will help us to think about the meaning of freedom in our present.

Rome and Roman: Slave Societies and Slaves in Society

To begin to describe the significance of slavery in Rome, I turn first to the terms used throughout this book – Rome and Roman, slavery and slave society. "Rome" refers to a place, a city on the Tiber River, and to the ancient state, one of many in Italy. By the mid-third century BCE, the Romans controlled the states and peoples of Italy south of the Po River. By the end of the second century BCE, Rome had conquered an empire and ruled overseas territories from the city of Rome (Maps 1 and 2). "Rome" and "Roman" are also used quite frequently to refer to the society and culture of the state of Rome. By the early first century BCE, this included people from all over Italy: they held citizenship in the Roman state, had adopted Roman social and cultural practices, and spoke Latin. In the first century CE, Roman citizenship was extended to individuals, peoples, and cities in Rome's overseas provinces, many of whom, like the Italians before them, had adopted Roman culture in a process called romanization. They, too, can be included in the terms Rome and Roman. In this book it will be clear from the context where Rome means the city, the state, or the society and where Roman refers to the culture and practices of Rome wherever they were lived out. For the most part, the focus of this book is on the heartland of the Roman empire, Italy, and parts of the western half of the empire.

Equally important is the term "slave society" and its distinction from a society that has slaves. In either case, the issue is chattel slavery: individual human beings are owned as property and treated as commodities that can be used, bought and sold, willed, given, or lent. Generally, historians define a slave society in quantitative terms: How many slaves? What proportion of the population were slaves? If the proportion of slaves is set at over 20 percent of the population, only five slave societies have existed in human history: ancient Greece, ancient Italy, and, in the modern period, the United States, Brazil, and the islands of the Caribbean. Many other societies have had chattel slaves but not in such numbers. In recent years, the number of slaves in the Roman empire and the proportion of slaves in the empire's population has been a subject of intense debate. Historians of ancient Rome lack the sources available to modern historians, so these numbers must rely on careful estimates and demographic models. The historian Walter Scheidel, whose work has been influential in the debate, estimates that slaves made up 10 percent of the empire's population – six million out of a population of some sixty million (a figure Scheidel calls a "lower limit"; 1997). However, as he and other scholars have argued, we must take account of geographical location and chronology in estimating the slave population. By the late first century BCE, in Roman Italy, the heartland of empire, slaves numbered 1 to 1.5 million out of a population of 5 to 6 million, or about 20–30 percent (Scheidel 2005). And it seems certain that these slaves were spread unequally throughout Italy itself. There were slaves in many other parts of the Roman empire but not in these numbers and perhaps, more importantly, not in the same "location" in the Roman economy.

Numbers are not the only or even the most important qualification of a slave society. M. I. Finley, the prominent social historian of ancient Greece and Rome, especially of ancient slavery, observed: "an assessment of the place of slaves in a society is not a matter of their totals, given a reasonably large number, but of their location, in two senses – first, who their owners were; secondly, what role they played, in the economy but not only in the economy" (1980: 80–81). In Roman Italy, although not in the entire Roman empire, slave labor produced most of the income of the wealthy by laboring on their farms and estates. There were free peasants and small landholders in the countryside, many of whom also added to the income of the rich as tenants and seasonal laborers. Slavery was only one form of dependent labor in the Roman world. Yet in one way the labor of slaves was critical for the elite: they served their owners as servants, administrators, financial agents, and

1. Funerary altar of Quintus Socconius Felix, Rome, c. 50–100 CE. A husband and wife in formal dress lie side by side on a dining couch behind a small table with drinking cups on it. Three long-haired boys dressed in elegant tunics (probably slaves) wait on them. One boy holds a jug, another a towel, and the third a garland. They signal both the wealth and taste of their owners. (Felbermeyer, Neg. D-DAI-Rom 1963.0755)

secretaries. As pointed out in Chapter 5, these domestic servants produced social status, not income, for their owners. They allowed their
owners to live nobly: they took care of their owners' physical needs,
symbolized slaveholders' social status, and, as property, displayed their
owners' wealth (Figure 1). Even after slaves were no longer the major
component of the rural labor force, slave domestic servants continued
to display their owners' preeminence (Figure 2). In ancient Rome,
then, elite wealth, status, and leisure were all built on the labor and
lives of slaves.

These concerns lead to a consideration of Roman culture – society's
values, attitudes, and ways of seeing itself and others. The ownership of
slaves was an expression of power because owners exercised almost total
control over their human property. As an expression of power – even a
model of domination – slavery had an importance beyond its economic
significance. Thus, for example, it became a useful metaphor for the

2. Painting of a wine server, Rome, first half of the fourth century CE. The painting from a building on the Caelian Hill dates to a period when slaves were no longer the primary work force on rural estates, although they continued to serve as domestic servants of all sorts. This servant, with a cup in one hand and a sieve in the other, has long elaborately curled hair and wears a fancy tunic decorated with circles and stripes and embroidered in red and gold. Servants like this man served to express the luxury, wealth, and hospitality of their owners. (Museo Nazionale, Photo: Soprintendenza Archeologica delle province di Napoli e Caserta)

lives of senators who felt disempowered by the rule of the emperors, especially bad emperors. Because slavery was considered a degrading condition, Roman satirists, poets, philosophers, and historians could label an individual or a behavior servile when they wanted to denigrate someone or some act. In short, slavery shaped the Roman mentality.

Slavery as Social Institution, Experience, and Lived Reality

Questions about the numbers of slaves, their roles in the economy, their place in Roman society, and the effects of slavery on Roman values and attitudes involve slavery as an institution. "Institution" means an organization of roles that include conduct – how people should behave or are imagined to behave. It refers, too, to a system of practices and ideas that are socially sanctioned and maintain the continued existence

3. Head of Cicero, Rome. (Alinari/Art Resource, New York)

of the institution. Focusing on slavery as an institution means stepping back from the discrete lives of thousands of individual slaves, their owners, and Romans who were not slaveholders but lived in a slave society. To inquire about the lives of one or three or ten of those thousands of slaves, owners, and other Romans is to ask about experience and about how the individual lived the institution. One slaveholder may have been kind, another cruel, and a third indifferent; one slave may have openly accepted his or her condition, another run away or caused trouble, and still another suffered his or her condition silently. In other words, when we look at experience, we find complexity and a wide variety of different situations. However, as argued throughout this study, the institution of slavery always shaped the experience of every slave.

An example helps to clarify the distinction between institution and experience. The famous orator Marcus Tullius Cicero (Figure 3) had a slave secretary and literary assistant named Tiro. Cicero freed Tiro in 54 BCE, and Tiro continued to work for his former owner until Cicero's death in 43 BCE. Letters to Tiro from Cicero, his brother Quintus, and his son Marcus testify to the family's concern, care, and affection for Tiro. Congratulating his brother when he freed Tiro,

Quintus remarks that Cicero preferred that Tiro should be the family's friend, not its slave (*Letters to Friends* 16.16.1). Yet as the classicist Mary Beard points out, the brothers continue to play on the language of service and slavery in their letters to the free Tiro (2002). Encouraging Tiro to recover from an illness, Cicero orders him "to be a slave to his body," meaning that he should put his body before everything else and take care of his health (16.4.4). In 44 BCE Quintus makes a joke about flogging: he has, he tells the former slave, flogged Tiro in his mind for not writing him (16.26.1). Twenty-first-century readers may find it difficult to see the humor in a joke about whipping addressed to a former slave. About Tiro's point of view, nothing is known, since there is no letter from him to the brothers, although in a letter written later in the year Quintus repeats the flogging imagery, commenting that in his letter Tiro has given him a whipping for his idleness (he had not written).

The joke about mental flogging belongs to the particular interchange of these men at a particular moment in Roman history. However, the joke derives its punch from the institution of slavery that defines the slave as property subject to the power of his owner. Roman masters could and did whip their slaves as a normal practice for failures of conduct and service or for no reason but the master's whim. Without Tiro's words, we can only guess at his experience of these jokes. Perhaps he gave back as good as he got. Here, even where we have the evidence for the complexities of a particular relationship of master and slave and can observe the intersection of institution and lived reality, we see them through the words of the master. The example of Tiro and Cicero, however, gives us a glimpse of the problem of position and point of view. Position, tempered by individuals' social power and place in the relations of slave and owner, informs their points of view – who sees what and who reports what, and the problem of point of view shapes our knowledge of slavery as an institution and slavery as experience. So it is useful to begin the study of Roman slavery by looking at the evidence for it. Another way to see the problem is to ask what story each of our sources tells and who tells that story.

The Sources for Roman Slavery

Historians look at four kinds of sources to understand Roman slavery: literature, law, inscriptions, and archaeological remains. Literature includes Latin and Greek texts, usually written by freeborn men, most often members of the social elite or at least of the propertied classes: it covers a wide variety of genres – history, poetry, satire, novels, plays, philosophical tracts, essays, letters, biographies, and speeches. Sometimes a text refers directly and explicitly to social realities – the facts of daily life; more often it refers to what we would see as imaginary situations. Novels invent their plots; satire relies on stereotypes; comedies are populated by stock characters; history recounts legend, rumor, and traditional tales. Speeches and biographies include invective, claims, and insults drawn from political rhetoric. Nonetheless, the texts make assumptions that tell us about Roman social life: even where the story and characters are fictional, they depict Roman attitudes, values, and ways of seeing.

Law refers most often to two major sources: the *Institutes* of Gaius, a sort of textbook of Roman law composed in the second century CE, and the *Digest* of Justinian, a compilation of Roman law put together in the early sixth century CE that preserves earlier laws, edicts, and imperial orders. The *Institutes* sets out the key principles and practices of Roman law; the *Digest* collects legal opinions on nearly every subject of Roman life. These legal texts usually outline the possibilities in Roman social life rather than state the facts of particular and actual cases. However, in outlining possibilities, law refers to the social world and hence to Roman slave society. Law describes the position of freeborn citizens, slaves, and freedmen; it sets out the family and property rights that belonged to the free and the disabilities suffered by the slave. In various ways, law articulates the honor of individuals with respect to others and the state, drawing clear connections between honor and power.

If we rely solely on law and literature for our understanding of Roman society, we rely on a story that excludes for the most part the position of slaves and of lower-class Romans. When legal and literary texts describe social reality, they do not truly represent the nonprivileged groups of Rome because they are, quite simply, not records written by those they describe. Law maps the boundaries within which action took place and the roles determined by rights and privileges from the perspective of jurists who owned property, including slaves. With few exceptions, where Roman writers speak directly about slaves and ex-slaves, they do so from the perspective of slaveholders and freeborn Romans. The figures of slave and freed slave in literature serve the descriptive, moral, or humorous purposes of their creators, and these literary slaves inscribe the values and attitudes of freeborn author and audience.

Two exceptions stand out. Phaedrus, a freed slave of the emperor Augustus, who wrote in the early first century CE, told fables, a genre often associated with slaves or those without power. At key points in his fables, he accounts for the perspective of slaves – one that he knew from his own experience. The comic poet Plautus who composed his comedies in the late third and early second centuries BCE, too, may be counted as an exception. His audience included both slaves and free people, and scholars argue about where in these comedies and if in these comedies Plautus conveys a slave point of view. However, for most Roman writers and jurists, we can say that although they account for slaves in certain ways, they tend to cast into the shadows the experience of those they dominated. Because these authors were often slaveholders, law and literature tell us most about the institution of slavery and the experience of masters, and least about the experience of slaves.

Potentially, inscriptions fill this gap. Romans of all classes inscribed a wide variety of texts on stone: dedications to gods; declarations honoring emperors, officials, and private individuals; the acts of senators, emperors, and private benefactors; regulations of various sorts including the punishment of slaves or the rules of occupational, burial, or religious associations; and epitaphs. Some of these inscriptions record the actions of men and women whose experience is excluded from law and literature. Dedications to gods, emperors, officials, and private individuals document benefactions, gratitude for benefits bestowed, or the hopes of future favors. In epitaphs, the living remember the dead. Within the limits of a conventional vocabulary, slaves, freedmen, and ordinary freeborn citizens alike represented themselves. We can ask: in light of the conditions set by law, how did these individuals and groups present themselves?

The following chapters often use epitaphs to speak for slaves and freed slaves. Although they belong to the world of the dead, they refer to a lived social reality. In Rome death was followed by prescribed rituals that purified the living, gave forms for their grief, and commemorated the deceased. Stone epitaphs with the name of the deceased and often the commemorator were material markers of both the social rituals and personal experience of death. The wealthy, especially senators and aristocrats, were celebrated in elaborate funerals; large tombs and often lengthy epitaphs record their existence (Figure 4). Poor Romans were often buried in unmarked mass graves. The funerals, tombs, and epitaphs of everyone else included the grand and the humble: tombs range from small ash urns to large elaborate structures; epitaphs from plaques with only the deceased's name to elaborate accounts of the deceased's life or the commemorator's grief (Figure 5). But even the simplest plaque marked an individual's existence (see Figures 44 and 46). The epitaph also made the dead present for the living during the yearly public festivals and private ceremonies that took place at the tomb. The audience was the deceased's family, friends, and associates, although some epitaphs self-consciously address a wider circle of people, even the men or women who happened to pass by on their journey on one of the roads outside a Roman city: Stop and read, command such epitaphs. In a way foreign to most modern funerary practices, ceremony and epitaph tried to fix a social place for the dead in the society of the living.

Although the epitaphs of slaves worked within certain conventions not reserved only for slaves, these epitaphs can be seen as testimony of the perceptions and experience of their slave authors. This use poses

4. Tombs of Caecilia Metella (a) and Gaius Cestius (b), Rome, late first century BCE. These two large tombs belonged to members of the senatorial elite and reflected the power and wealth of the deceased and their families. (Courtesy of Emma-Jayne Graham)

5. Tombs of the poor, Isola Sacra, Ostia. At one of the cemeteries for the port of Ostia, behind the tombs of those with property, are the burials of the poor. (a) Amphorae mark graves (the ashes of the dead). (b) Between two graves is the burial of a body (inhumation) covered by tiles tilted against each other. (Fototeca Unione, American Academy in Rome)

its own problems of interpretation. Because most epitaphs offer only the barest facts of a slave's life, they pale in comparison with the juicy details found in literature. Historians can color in the outlines by paying careful attention to the authorship of epitaphs, their context, and their audiences as well as by drawing on the literary and legal sources for information on the facts of a life named in an epitaph. The problem is always what and how we fill in: on the one side is the danger of filling in too much, and on the other is saying nothing at all. Nevertheless, this information often provides the most direct access to the experience and perspective of an individual; the evidence of death becomes a mirror that reflects how men and women saw themselves in life.

The study of ancient objects, art, and ruins contributes to our understanding of the physical life of slaves as well as the Roman representation of slaves. Archaeologists have uncovered a wide range of material: the remains of Roman houses, villas, shops, bars, and larger scale workshops such as bakeries and fulleries (cloth cleaning and treatment workshops); images of war captives, slaves, and ex-slaves; representations of work; and even the fetters used to restrain captives during transport and some slaves working in different circumstances. Roman material culture, like other sources for Roman slavery, presents problems. It is often difficult to identify individual men, women, or children as slaves in sculpture, reliefs, and paintings. Archaeologists have often found the service areas of Roman houses, where we would expect to find slaves (Figure 6), but identifying a house's slave quarters has proved more troublesome. Nonetheless, ancient representations, objects, and ruins depict slaves and freed slaves themselves or reveal the places and conditions of their work and the spaces in which they carried on their social lives.

The example of cooks illustrates the possibilities and limitations of these four kinds of sources. The stories they tell often reinforce one another, and, at the same time, they often do not line up neatly. Slave cooks are found in Roman literature, law, and epitaphs, and we can imagine them in their places of work in the ruins of Roman houses. In Roman literature, cooks appear fairly often as stock characters in

6. Service area and its *lararium* in the House of the Vetti (VI.15.1), Pompeii. The service area of the house (marked by hatching on the plan) (b) has its own atrium (hall) with a *lararium* (c), a shrine with a painting of the household's *lares* (household deities) and the *genius* (guardian spirit) of the head of the household and owner of the slaves who worked in the house (a). Thus, decoration put the slaveholder near the work areas and perhaps the quarters for some of his slaves. (a: Courtesy of Andrew Wallace-Hadrill; b: from J. R. Clarke, *Art in the Lives of Ordinary Romans* [Berkeley: University of California Press, 2003], p. 98, fig. 51; c: Photo Michael Larvey su concessione del Minstero per i Beni e le Attività Culturali – Soprintendenza Speciale per i Beni Archeologici di Napoli e Pompei)

Roman comedy, as signs of luxury and decadence, and as part of the household staff that served propertied Romans. In law, cooks figure as slaves in legacies, dowries, and calculations of the "equipment" necessary for running a house or farming a piece of land. Cooks show up in the epitaphs from the city of Rome. Many of the houses of the wealthy in Pompeii included a kitchen for the preparation of food where cooks would have worked and, possibly, lived.

Passages from the ancient Roman historian Livy and the poet Martial illustrate the representation of the slave cook in literature. For Livy, writing in the late first century BCE, the slave cook belongs to a story about Roman luxury:

> For the beginnings of foreign luxury were introduced into the City by the army from Asia. They for the first time imported into Rome couches of bronze, valuable robes for coverlets, tapestries and other products of the loom, and what at the time was considered luxurious furniture – tables with one pedestal and sideboards. Then female players of the lute and harp and other festal delights of entertainments were made adjuncts to banquets; the banquets themselves, moreover, began to be planned with both greater care and greater expense. At that time the cook, to the ancient Romans the most worthless of slaves (*vilissimum … mancipium*), both in their judgment of values and in the use they made of him, began to have value, and what had been merely a necessary service (*ministerium*) came to be regarded as an art (*ars*). Yet those things which were then looked upon as remarkable were hardly even the germs of luxury to come. (Livy, *History of Rome* 39.6.7, trans. Evan T. Sage, *LCL*)

Livy's account of the return of the Roman army from Asia Minor in 187 BCE moves from things (clothes and furnishings) to people (female lute and harp players and cooks) – logically from a Roman point of view because the people Livy mentions were slaves and, like furniture, were commodities that could be bought and sold. Livy's language makes this clear when he calls the old-time slave cook "the most worthless *mancipium,*" a word used of slaves but also of other property. What Livy does not quite say is that slaves, like things, were part of the plunder seized by Roman armies in their conquest of the Mediterranean. The cook is singled out for special comment: Romans of earlier times had considered his work a simple, everyday service, where luxury in Livy's day made this ordinary employment an art. It is difficult to see Livy's account as a factual history of slave cooks because his interpretation repeats the common Roman perception that the wealth garnered in Rome's conquests created a problem of luxury, a luxury that was foreign and counter to the traditional Roman value of simplicity in daily life. However, this Roman interpretation – that as the meals became fancier, so the households and possessions (including cooks) of the wealthy became more elaborate and luxurious – enlarges our understanding of the Roman institution of slavery: we can see the workings of Roman elite logic that considered slaves as things, and we can glimpse how slaves can be used to talk about concerns other than slavery.

An epigram (short poem) written by Martial more than a century later elaborates the meaning of slave as property:

> I seem to you savage and too fond of choice food (too much the epicure) because on account of the dinner, Rusticus, I beat my cook. If that seems to you a trivial reason for a flogging, for what reason, then, do you wish a cook to be beaten? (8.23)

Here the slave cook is beaten for a poorly prepared meal: as property, the slave, even if his work is considered an art, has no physical integrity and is subject to his owner's physical violence. Martial's words, too, reduce the person of the slave cook to his function: cooks cook; if they do not, beat them – as you would an ox that does not perform his assigned task.

Like Livy, who makes the slave cook a sign of Roman luxury, Martial, too, uses the slave cook to comment not on slaves or cooks per se but on Roman values and attitudes. "Rusticus" is a name used by Martial for its basic meaning. The adjective *rusticus* can refer to a country bumpkin who lacks urban refinement, but the name also may evoke some of the principles of Stoicism, a Greek philosophy adapted by certain upper-class Romans. Roman Stoics urged their followers to live simply, to avoid excess, and to pay little attention to their physical desires. A famous Stoic senator during the reign of the emperor Nero was named Rusticus: he wrote a biography of an even more famous Stoic senator and was killed by the emperor Domitian in 93 CE. If Martial's use of the name Rusticus identifies his addressee as a man of Stoic principles, the poet ridicules the Stoic criticism that men who are overly interested in food are slaves to their appetites. Martial's reduction of the cook to his function dismisses the complaint that the speaker in the poem is cruel and overly concerned with his palate.

Roman law talks about the slave cook in more dispassionate terms than literature, but it, too, views the slave as property. In the following passage from the *Digest,* the concern of the jurist is how to determine which slave goes to which heir:

> If someone is transferred from a job (*officium*) to a craft (*artificium*), as when a litter-bearer later becomes a cook, some rightly think the legacy is extinguished because the job is replaced by the craft. But this does not apply in reverse. If one slave knows several crafts and cooks have been bequeathed to one person, weavers to another, litter-bearers to another, the slave must be said to go to the one to whom the practitioners of the craft with which he is most familiar have been bequeathed. (32.1.65.1–2, trans. A. Watson)

The jurist goes on to talk about slave hairdressers and then without pause passes on to herd animals: distinguishing among litter bearers, cooks, and hairdressers gives way to the distinctions between pigs, oxen, horses, and sheep. Where Livy includes cooks among furnishings as items of luxury, Roman legal logic puts cooks in line with animals, which count equally as inheritable property. Law gives us a similar but less charged distinction than Livy's "necessary service" and "art": the litter bearer performs an *officium,* the cook an *artificium* – a distinction that depends of the acquisition of skills. The lawyers assume, too, that a litter bearer could become a cook or that a slave might know several trades.

The epitaph of Zena – who is identified by his occupation and not his legal status as a slave – is mute, compared to Livy's history and Martial's epigram (for similar epitaphs from the same tomb, see Figures 44 and 46):

ZENA
COOK (*Corpus of Latin Inscriptions* 6.6249, Rome)

Context and other information help to fill in the story this inscription tells, but what we can say remains speculative. Still, the attempt is important because, however mute, the stone brings us to the life of a real cook who lived in the late first century BCE or early first century CE. The small plaque marked a niche for an ash urn in a tomb set aside for the slaves and freed slaves of the noble family of the Statilii Tauri. The tomb, called by modern scholars a *columbarium* (a chamber filled with such plaques and niches), was on the Via Praenestina-Labicana, near the Porta Praenestina (the modern Porta Maggiore): it consisted of three rooms whose walls were filled with hundreds of niches and plaques like Zena's (see Figure 7 for an example of a *columbarium*).

The tomb and its burials were administered by a burial club or society composed of the slaves and freed slaves of the Statilii. They participated not only in the funerary rites but also in commemorative festivals for the dead. We should imagine the walls of niches and plaques decorated with wreaths and the chamber itself littered with the remains of banquets. As Zena had lived and worked with other slaves, so he was buried with them. In this particular tomb, many of his fellow

7. *Columbarium* of the Vigna Codini, Rome.

slaves, too, noted their jobs. Zena the cook, then, was commemorated in the midst of other cooks, foot servants, provisioners, hairdressers, and others. We cannot know if "cook" expressed Zena's pride in his job or his position in some hierarchy of jobs in the household, as some scholars believe, but clearly his work identified him to the audience of his fellow slaves among whom he had lived and worked.

In Roman houses and villas, we can see where the slaves like Zena did some of the work of cooking. The House of the Menander was one of the grandest in Pompeii before the city was buried in ash by the eruption of Mount Vesuvius in 79 CE (Figure 8). Its kitchen, like kitchens in other large houses, was segregated from the more public areas of the house – including the rooms where the owner and his guests ate the food prepared by the likes of Zena (although some preparations were done on braziers near the dining areas). In the House of the Menander, the kitchen can be reached only from a long dog-leg corridor (M and M1, Figure 9) off the peristyle (courtyard/garden surrounded by a portico) (Figure 8). As in other houses, the kitchen was located near a latrine (Room 26), flushed by dirty water from the

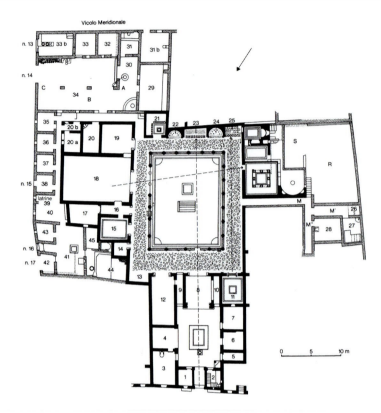

8. Plan of the House of the Menander (I.10.4), Pompeii. (From J. R. Clarke, *The Houses of Roman Italy, 100 BC–AC 250* [Berkeley: University of California Press, 1991], p. 15, fig. 6)

kitchen. The relatively small space (4 × 3 meters) included the typical elements of a Roman kitchen: a hearth (on the north end of the room), a work surface, and a sink (in the southwest corner) (Figure 10). Near the hearth was a *lararium* painting that can no longer be seen. The *lares* were household deities who protected the householder, his family, and his slaves, and such *lararia* were the sites of ritual observance. In the House of the Menander, as in other houses in Pompeii, they looked over the preparation of food.

Cooking was done on the top of a hearth (the arched openings below were used to store wood or charcoal): pottery and bronze vessels

9. Dog-leg corridor (M and M1) in the House of the Menander (I.10.4), Pompeii.

were placed directly on top of a charcoal fire or on metal stands. By the time of the house's destruction, the room was open to the air, although earlier it seems to have been roofed. In most cases, Roman kitchens were dark and poorly ventilated, so the cook worked in a small room full of fumes and smoke. From the archaeological remains of kitchens, we see something of the lives of Livy's valued slave cook whose menial work had become an art, Martial's beaten cook who has been punished for an ill-prepared meal, the *Digest*'s cook whose craft distinguishes who will inherit him, and Zena, slave of the Statilii, whose small epitaph identifies him by his job. All spent (or must be imagined to have spent) hours in small rooms, dirtied by smoke and the odors of cooked food, refuse, and the nearby latrine and crowded with assistants and waiters carrying dishes in and out.

10. Kitchen in the House of the Menander (I.10.4), Room 27, Pompeii. (Courtesy of Roger Ling)

Although we can imagine a slave cook in a Pompeian kitchen, the archaeological site tells us little about the slave's personality or tastes. In contrast to other areas of the house where paintings, mosaics, and attention to light and views catered to the tastes and pleasures of the house's owners, the kitchen was designed for production, not for a particular person. Potentially, of course, slaves could remake the kitchen as their own. Yet when a *lararium* in or near the kitchen had an image of the spirit of the owner, the shrine did more than provide divine protection; it reminded the slaves in the kitchen of their owner's presence, his claim to the space, and their duty to him (compare Figure 6).

The perspectives of these four kinds of sources tell us a great deal about Roman slavery. The literary and legal sources illustrate the institutional nature of the slaveholder's power and speak to the centrality of slaves in creating cultural niceties like gourmet food. The epitaph, even in its relative muteness, offers hints about a slave's views. And the archaeological site helps us to appreciate the space of a slave's everyday life. Aside from the content of each, their form – the volubility of the literary texts and law and the inarticulateness of the slave's epitaph – speaks volumes about the nature of institutionalized power in ancient Roman slavery.

Reading *Slavery in the Roman World*

Each of the following chapters weaves together literature, law, inscriptions, and material culture to look at the intersection of slavery as a Roman social institution and slavery as an experience – in other words, the macro-level of social structure and the micro-level of the men and women, free and slave, who lived Roman history. To foster attention to institution and experience, most chapters begin with two quotations that set side by side the words of slave owners and those of slaves (or passages that articulate the owner's concerns and passages that spell out the conditions of the slave). These chapters are roughly circular, moving from the nitty-gritty details of daily life to the larger, more comprehensive view of institutions and social structure and returning to the experience or lived realities of slaves. Although each chapter can be read independently, the chapters build on each other, so that the issues covered in one chapter raise questions that will be answered by the next. Chapter 2 outlines the Roman social order, locates slaves in Roman society, and traces the history of slavery at Rome. Chapter 3 describes the Roman slave trade and tries to reconstruct the experience of persons who were sold. Chapter 4 examines owners' views of their slaves and their own behavior as masters; it then turns to what this meant for the lives of enslaved men, women, and children. Chapter 5 takes the question of lived conditions and experience further by focusing on work. It looks at slaves in three settings: the rural estate, the large urban household of the social elite, and the shops and artisanal workshops in the city.

CHAPTER 2

THE ROMAN SOCIAL
ORDER AND A
HISTORY OF SLAVERY

Manumissions also belong to the law of nations (*ius gentium*). Manumission means sending out of one's hand, that is, granting freedom. For whereas one who is in slavery is subject to the hand (*manus*) and power of another, on being sent out of hand he is freed of that power. All of which originated from the *ius gentium,* since, of course, everyone would be born free by the natural law, and manumission would not be known when slavery was unknown. But after slavery came in by the *ius gentium,* there followed the boon (*beneficium*) of manumission. And thenceforth, we all being called by the one natural name "men," in the *ius gentium* there came to be three classes: free men, and set against those slaves and the third class, freedmen, that is, those who had stopped being slaves. (*Digest* 1.1.4, trans. A. Watson)

The Roman jurist Ulpian identifies three types of people in a historical account in which natural law (*ius naturale*) gives way to the law of nations (*ius gentium*). In his view, all humans living in a world of natural law are just "men": slavery is unknown, so all are free. Humans living under the law of nations – in a world of states, societies, and slavery, are divided into three groups: freeborn people, slaves, and freedmen (slaves freed by manumission, the Roman term for freeing a slave). In fact, individuals in Roman society were distinguished by legal status: Ulpian's terms – freeborn, slave, and freed slave – name very real differences of rights, duties, and privileges with respect to the state and other individuals. The history of these distinctions is considerably more complex than Ulpian's cursory sketch suggests.

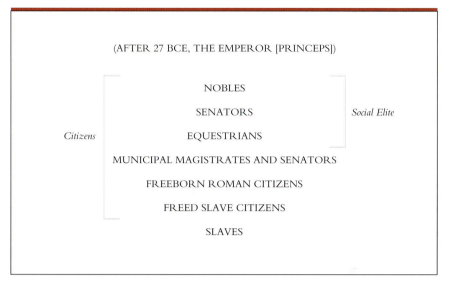

11. The Roman social order

Some groups do not fit easily into this chart:

(a) *Augustales,* boards of freedmen dedicated to the worship of the emperor, were wealthy and had rank in their local communities, although they were still ex-slaves.

(b) Rich freed slaves were wealthier than most ordinary Roman citizens, although they could still be ridiculed as ex-slaves.

(c) The emperor's slaves and freedmen (called the *familia Caesaris*) had privileges and often power, although they were slaves and ex-slaves.

This chapter locates slaves within Roman society and history. The chapter begins with a survey of the Roman social order in the first century BCE and first century CE. By "social order," I mean not only legal status but also social standing that measures how individuals ranked in Roman society with respect to others with the same legal status. Some freeborn Romans were wealthy, powerful, and specially regarded by their social inferiors; others were poor, relatively powerless, and undistinguished. The division between the social elite and ordinary citizens shaped the social order in which slavery flourished at Rome and in which slaves lived and worked (Figure 11). Central to both legal status and social status is the question of command and obedience: this section then maps who in Roman society did and could command and who obeyed. The political history that shaped this social order and Roman slavery is briefly recounted in the next section. Especially important is the development of Rome's large-scale slave system as Rome conquered the Mediterranean and expanded its empire.

The Roman Social Order and Legal Status

Roman Citizens (Common People or Plebs)

All freeborn Romans were citizens of the state, although wealth and social status divided ordinary freeborn Romans from a social elite of senators, nobles, and equestrians. Citizenship gave every citizen certain rights and claims that defined him or her as a member of the community until in the late first century CE wealth, not citizenship, began to determine legal rights and privileges. Until that point, citizenship guaranteed the physical integrity of every citizen, male and female.

The Roman citizen was free, but not from the authority of another. As a citizen, a man was supposed to obey the magistrates of the Roman state, as a soldier his general, and as a son his father. Traditionally, female citizens owed obedience to husbands as well as fathers. In fact, Romans viewed submission to authority within the family as proper and uniquely Roman. The paternal power (*patria potestas*) of the head of the family (*paterfamilias*) characterized proper Roman family order. Legally, the *paterfamilias* held the power of life and death (*ius vitae necisque*) over his children as well as his slaves. Indeed, the liabilities of the son or daughter in paternal power were similar to the slave's, although they were not as drastic and had different repercussions. Roman authors recount instances of children killed or physically punished, but, in practice, fathers and mothers whipped their slaves, not their children, and educational tracts strongly advise against whipping freeborn children. Unlike the slave's, the child's position was considered an honorable one because he or she owed obedience to a father, not a master. Moreover, the freeborn child succeeded to the father's position and property, at least in cases of inheritance where the father did not leave a will.

12. Painting of "Terentius Neo and his Wife" (VII.2.6), Pompeii. Scholars have debated the identity and status of this man and woman, but, whoever they were, it seems that the couple were ordinary citizens of the city of Pompeii. Both hold signs of their literacy – she a stylus and he a scroll. (Photo Michael Larvey su concessione del Minstero per i Beni e le Attività Culturali – Soprintendenza Speciale per i Beni Archeologici di Napoli e Pompei)

Male citizens must be distinguished from female citizens (Figure 12). Every male citizen had the right to vote (until the Roman voting assemblies disappeared under the rule of the emperors), to control his property, to marry, and to have legitimate children who were also Roman citizens. A female citizen, too, could contract a proper

Roman marriage and have children who were citizens and therefore members of the community. On the death of a *paterfamilias,* the citizen was legally independent (*sui iuris*) and in charge of his or her own life and property (including slaves). A male citizen became not only *sui iuris* but also a *paterfamilias* in his own right, gaining paternal power over his own children. Paternal power passed from one generation to the next, securing a legitimate place in society for fathers and sons. The male citizen released from paternal power took control of his property and could make contracts binding in Roman law; he became legally responsible for his own actions and had legal recourse in the courts against those who injured him or his family or damaged his property. Unlike her male counterpart, a woman always had a guardian, a man who gave approval to all her legal acts, although various devices reduced the limitations of this practice. Last, a woman of citizen status did not vote or serve on juries; she could not sue on behalf of others; and although she could sue on her own behalf, she rarely appeared in court.

All freeborn people were defined by their physical integrity. Citizenship protected the freeborn from summary execution, flogging, chaining, imprisonment, and torture. The right of appeal guaranteed the physical integrity of citizens in interactions with the state and its officials. Lawsuits for what the Romans called injury or outrage (*iniuria*) allowed citizens to defend their person and honor and that of the family against the offenses of others. Injury or outrage affected both individuals' bodies and their social standing. In effect, injury resulted when one person asserted his power against another, especially in a physical act: striking a person with a stick, fist, or sword; flogging him; forcibly entering his home; preventing him from fishing in the sea, catching birds, bathing publicly, taking a seat in the theater, or associating with others in public; or advertising someone's property for sale as if he were a debtor. Someone insulted a proper Roman woman by behaving in a lewd manner toward her or calling out to her on the street. Thus, the honor of the freeborn was tied to their physical integrity. A physical assertion of power offended its victims because it ignored their status as freeborn citizens and treated them like slaves, those who were powerless and physically vulnerable. Failure to recognize that an individual had integrity denied his or her membership in the community.

Senators and Nobles

The gap between ordinary Roman citizens, the common people or the plebs, and their social betters – senators, nobles, and equestrians – was one of wealth, social prestige, and political power. Men in the senatorial class (or, in Roman terms, the senatorial order) were the most politically powerful members of Roman society, and they had the most social prestige (Figure 13). In part, their position depended on wealth. Land was the basis of wealth in Roman society, and because land was inherited, so was social standing and political power. Empire brought new sources of wealth in the form of plunder, slaves, taxes, gifts, and bribes; this wealth greatly enriched the senatorial class. By the second century BCE, enslaved war captives farmed senators' land and served in their households.

Social standing derived from political power. Men with such status held office, led Rome's armies, and sat in the senate, the most powerful body in the Roman state. Within the senatorial class, there was a still more exclusive group, the nobility. A man was a noble if he or some ancestor had held the consulship, the highest office in the Roman state. The power of the nobility, in fact, was expressed institutionally in holding office and dominating the decisions of the senate. Although assemblies of ordinary citizens elected magistrates and passed laws, senators and nobles directed the Roman state and society. Thus, historians talk about Rome until the late first century BCE as an oligarchy (the rule of a few). The rule of the emperors beginning in the late first century BCE ended senators' and nobles' political monopoly. Although they continued to hold office, sit in the senate, govern provinces, and even command troops, they did so under the control of the emperor.

13. Noble with the busts of his ancestors, Rome, late first century BCE. (Faraglia, Neg. D-DAI-Rom 1937.0378)

But the social prestige of this class remained, and so, too, their wealth and need to live nobly.

Equestrian Order

Below senators and nobles in rank were a class (order) called the equestrians, although the distinction between senators and equestrians was not always economic. Like senators, they, too, owned land, farmed their estates with slave labor, and benefited by the conquests that led to empire. Some members of equestrian order met the property requirement to hold office; others were even wealthier than senators. In fact, ambitious sons of equestrian families ran for office and entered the senatorial order, so the senate was constantly replenished by the equestrian order.

Generally, however, equestrian men chose not to run for office and sit in the senate – which is not to say they had no role in politics. They had a determinative vote in the assembly that elected the higher offices, including the consulship. In the second century BCE, they also began to sit on the juries of law courts that tried public crimes such as public violence, election bribery, and extortion in the provinces. Equestrians' role as jurors in the extortion court that tried provincial governors was especially important for their own interests. Until the late first century BCE, a group of equestrians, called *publicani,* collected the taxes of empire, a source of great profits for these men, and senatorial governors who inhibited their activities were frequently themselves accused of extortion when they returned to Rome after their term in the provinces. These activities ceased under the rule of the emperors, but equestrians, like senators, maintained their social prestige and found other roles in the military and government.

Since social standing was limited by birth and property, and since the distribution of wealth in Roman society was extremely unequal, so, too, was the distribution of prestige. In principle, the law favored free over slave, citizen over free noncitizen, freeborn citizen over freed citizen. However, throughout Roman history, the political and social elite lorded it over their social inferiors: ordinary Roman citizens provided the manpower of Roman armies, labor in the countryside, and followers in politics. By the late first century CE, inequalities of wealth and rank produced further inequalities in legal privilege. The poor and the lowly were tried in different courts and received harsher punishments than the socially prominent. The resources of the wealthy also enabled more extensive and effective use of the legal system, including the right of appeal. Judges and magistrates, members of their class, were biased toward them. However, even if they lacked privilege and power in relation to their social betters, all freeborn citizens could identify themselves as members of the community and as members of a family whose relations were acknowledged in law and practice. These claims distinguished freeborn citizens from slaves.

Slaves

Legally, the slave was *res,* a thing, property, an object. Roman law acknowledges slaves as people and distinguishes human property from other kinds of property, although at times the distinction is difficult to see (Figures 14a and b). The slave, like a piece of land, an animal, or an inanimate object, could be sold, lent, mortgaged, given away, or bequeathed in a will. As property, slaves lacked all that defined freeborn Roman citizens: legitimate kinship relations acknowledged in law and by society, physical integrity, the ability to set law in motion on their own behalf, and the ownership of property. Although Roman slave owners incorporated slaves into their households in various ways, the slave, whether a captive seized in war or a person born into slavery in Rome (*verna*), was seen as an outsider. In the following discussion of these conditions, it is useful to consider their collective effect: slave men and women lived their lives inside Roman society, but that society, like other slave societies, defined them as socially dead – without rights, family, and membership in the legitimate social order (see Patterson 1982).

Slaves seized in Rome's wars abroad lost their ethnic or national heritage; slaves born in Roman society were not considered Romans and so had no official ethnicity from birth. The Romans recognized the origins of slaves but in a way that made ethnicity a personal characteristic. The edict on the sale of slaves, for example, required that sellers state the origin (*natio*) of every slave put up for sale because the slave's personal qualities were in part judged by *natio:* "It is assumed that some slaves are good, because they come from a people (*natio*) which does not have a bad reputation, and others are thought to be bad because they come from a people which has a rather bad name" (*Digest*

14. (a) Sarcophagus of Caecilius Valianus, Rome, c. 270 CE. (Anger, Neg.
D-DAI-Rom 1990.0413) (b) Relief with banqueters, Pizzoli, mid-first century
CE. (G. Fittschen, Neg. D-DAI-Rom 1984VW0935) On the third-century
sarcophagus (a), the deceased reclines on a dining couch, surrounded and attended
by his servants, probably slaves: the seated woman plays an instrument; behind her a
woman holds a jar for wine or perfume. At the sides of the scene, young men with
long hair and in long-sleeved tunics carry food or items for hand washing. In death,
the servants wait on their owner and inscribe his imagined social standing. On the
earlier relief (b, probably part of a tomb), two distinct groups of diners – one
reclining on couches as at a formal banquet and the other seated on stools – are
attended by two servants in tunics. One carries wine to the formal diners, and the
other works at a table. Here servants/slaves are merely background to the activities
of the diners.

21.1.31.21). The term "people" does not signal a set of beliefs or practices lived out in a particular place among one's fellows: "good" and
"bad" are categories determined by the sellers and buyers of human
property and, as such, measure the slave's potential utility and obedience to a slaveholder.

Slaves' status as outsiders was furthered by their lack of socially acknowledged kin. Slave men and women, of course, had parents, spouses, and children, but neither Roman law nor Roman owners accepted slaves' familial relations as legitimate. Society did not recognize slave spouses as husband and wife but called them "tent mates" (*contubernales*); slave marriage was granted as a privilege by the slave owner, which could be withdrawn whenever he or she liked, without consideration of the slave spouses themselves. Law took into account slave motherhood because slave children belonged to their mother's owner; however, the issue was not parenthood but ownership, for whoever owned the slave woman at the time she gave birth was generally the owner of her child. Socially and legally, no male slave could be a father, and no slave, male or female, legally had a father. Roman slave owners could sell, will, loan, or trade their slave property as they wished; so, in principle, the slave family had no stability as a social unit, and, in fact, slave spouses as well as slave parents and children were often separated by the decisions of their owners.

Ownership, the relationship of slaveholder and slave, was the only socially and legally acknowledged relationship a slave had. Legally, slave owners had the power of life and death over their slaves and complete control of their slaves' productivity – "whatever is acquired through the slave, is acquired for the master," states the law (Gaius, *Institutes* 1.52). In other words, slaveholders controlled the physical existence of their human property. The control of the owner meant the loss of physical integrity for the slave. Slave men and women were beaten because they failed to do their jobs, refused to work, irritated a crabby master, or became outlets for an owner's frustration. The loss of physical integrity also meant sexual vulnerability for both male and female slaves. Law and literature refer quite often to the master's "boy," to slaveholders' advances on their male and female domestic servants, to the purchase of slaves for sexual relations, and to the alteration of a male slave's physical appearance (long hair) and body (castration) for sexual purposes. In the wider society, the physical vulnerability expressed in the slave's sexual use and abuse dishonored the victim. As noted above, the law on injury or outrage (*iniuria*) protected the physical integrity and honor of freeborn citizen women; forced sexual relations with a freeborn male were illegal, for the man who was penetrated was dishonored.

Enslaved people had no physical integrity and honor. Unlike the freeborn, slaves could not personally suffer *iniuria* – at least in the view of Roman lawyers. In cases that involved a slave, the honor of the slaveholder was abused by what amounted to an assault on an extension of himself. Wounding or killing a slave was usually counted as damage to property; the owner, not the slave, sued for the recovery of a loss to property. The state, too, treated the slave as physically vulnerable. Slave testimony was taken under torture, a treatment that, at least until the second century CE, was used exclusively for slaves, and like noncitizen foreigners, they endured punishments such as crucifixion and burning alive.

Despite this denial of the slave's integrity, slaves participated in various economic activities and businesses on behalf of their owners and sometimes themselves. They made contracts that were legally binding, participated in all sorts of transactions involving property, and paid for actions that caused offense, damage, or loss to others. Like sons in paternal power, some slaves had control of property, called a *peculium*: it could include monies, a business, personal items, and even slaves. Ultimately, however, the slave owner was responsible for the slave's actions, and, legally, the *peculium* belonged to the owner, who could take it away at will. In general, whether the slaveholder sued for acts committed against his or her slave or another sued the slaveholder for actions taken by his or her slave, the slave, unlike the son, appears in law as an extension of the slaveholder's will or person, or simply as his property.

Freedmen and Freedwomen (Freed Slaves)

Manumission (freeing a slave) was a common practice in Roman society (Figure 15). Roman authors often complain that there were too

15. Relief of the freed slaves of the Furius family, Rome, late first century BCE. The five freed slaves were manumitted by three different owners: the three women were freed by a Furia; the man, second from the left, by a Publius Furius; and the man at the far right by a Gaius Sulpicius. The exact relations among the five ex-slaves and among their ex-masters are unknown – in the former case, the probabilities are determined by their pose and name forms and in the latter by their name forms. (Alinari/Art Resource, New York)

many freed slaves in Roman society, and modern scholars debate the frequency of manumission and the numbers of slaves freed. As we shall see, certain slaves could expect manumission, and others had little hope of freedom. For slaves in general, however, the existence of freed slaves in society held out the possibility that slavery might have an end.

In terms of the slave's social death, manumission was a sort of social "rebirth" (although not a complete one). It not only terminated the slave's status as property; for slaves freed by citizen-owners, it also meant Roman citizenship with its attendant rights (Figure 16). Freed slaves could contract a proper Roman marriage recognized in law; they could have legally acknowledged children who themselves were citizens. Freed slaves could sell or transfer property, write a will, make contracts binding in their own name, and sue and be sued in their own right. Yet the citizenship of ex-slaves was hampered by legal and social disabilities that freeborn citizens did not endure. Most importantly, their servile past was a social stigma, and a continued relationship with their former owners placed limitations on ex-slaves' actions and behavior.

Freedom did not return the slave's lost ethnic heritage or parents. Unlike freeborn citizens, freed slaves could not inherit their father's culture. If they had been captured in a foreign war, they could not

16. Relief from the Tomb of the Haterii, Rome, first century CE. The deceased woman lies on a funeral couch with the tablets of her will at her feet. A male servant places a garland around her neck, and her two daughters beat their breasts in grief. Various mourners surround the couch – a female flute player, a female dirge singer, and men and women who may have been the woman's slaves or ex-slaves. Four grieving women, freed slaves, wear cone-shaped hats (*pillei*), the symbol of their manumission. (Schwanke, Neg. D-DAI-Rom 1981.2858)

practice their culture's values in Roman society without facing the stigma of alienness. If they had been born in slavery in Italy itself, they knew only the culture of their Roman owners or that created by their fellow slaves. Roman authors ridicule freedmen for having no birthdays and no fathers. The lack of a socially acknowledged father dishonored the ex-slave and left him open to mockery. Any freedman who acquired some wealth, the very basis of rank in Roman society, might find himself shamed by the jibe that he was illegitimate. The ridicule extended to ex-slaves' attempts to live as Romans in society. Roman authors, Martial, Juvenal, and Petronius, for example, depict these attempts as the base aping of aliens and characterize the values and behavior of ex-slaves who aspire to respectability as shabby and shallow.

A socially and legally acknowledged relationship with his or her former owner, too, circumscribed the life of the freed slave. The former owner, now patron, no longer had the right of life and death over the ex-slave and total control of the ex-slave's labor and goods, but the relationship shaped (or was supposed to shape) the freed slave's behavior to the patron's advantage. The grant of freedom by the slaveholder was considered a favor or kindness (*beneficium*) for which the freed slave was expected to show gratitude (Figure 17). The appropriate behavior was called *obsequium;* more than proper respect, the term denotes a compliance and accommodation to the will of another.

Roman law spells out the prescribed behavior that *obsequium* imposed on freed slaves in dealing with their patrons. Physical and verbal aggression was forbidden; even reproaching a patron was an offense to *obsequium*. Freed slaves' legal recourse against their former owners was restricted lest that recourse inhibit ex-slaves' required deference. In general, freed slaves needed the permission of a magistrate even to sue their patrons. Rarely did the magistrate allow a freed slave to sue his patron for injury or outrage – and then only in the most severe cases. The limitation on suits for injury is important in terms of the physical integrity associated with Roman citizenship.

In effect, freed slaves gained the physical integrity that slaves lacked in relation to others, but apparently they could never fully claim it in relation to the ex-owner who once claimed their bodies. Instances where a patron used harsh words or even administered a "light beating," grounds for legal action by a freeborn Roman citizen, were not severe enough to merit the action for injury by a former slave. According to the jurist Ulpian, "the praetor should not endure the slave of yesterday, who today is free, to complain that his master has spoken abusively to him, or struck him lightly, or criticized him" (*Digest* 47.10.7.2). Ulpian justifies ex-slaves' limited redress against the abuses of patrons by

17. Epitaph of Varia Servanda, Isola Sacra, Ostia, second century CE. On the back wall of the tomb of the Varii, at the base of a small shrine (a), is the epitaph of Varia Servanda, dedicated by two of her freed slaves (b). It reads: "To the Departed Spirits. For Varia Servanda, daughter of Publius. Her freed slaves, Ampelus and Ennychis, (made this plaque) with their own money." In their dedication the two ex-slaves express the appropriate gratitude to their former owner.

emphasizing freed slaves' servile past as property of the persons whom they now claim have dishonored them.

Because *obsequium* was defended by the threat of punishment administered by the patron or, if necessary, by the state, to antagonize the patron was dangerous. The legal system generally favored the patron, and incompliant ex-slaves could find themselves banished from a patron's favor or household or temporarily exiled from their city; in more serious cases, a magistrate could order a flogging or the confiscation of part of the freed slave's property. In the first century CE and later, severe offenses resulted in the loss of freedom. A patron's ill-humor or anger brought another element of vulnerability to the ex-slave's position when it was directed at the ex-slave, for the patron's actions depended as much on the patron's own self-control as on the freed slave's behavior. Some freed slaves no doubt revered their patrons, but both literature and law see fear as a motive for good behavior; Roman jurists point to fear as well as excessive reverence to explain cases of former slaves' undue subjection to their former owners.

Patrons had a claim to their ex-slaves' labor, especially through services called *operae,* workdays for which a sum of money could be substituted. Negotiated before manumission and confirmed by oath afterwards, *operae* in some cases became so onerous that jurists intervened to modify the obligations of freed slaves to work for their patrons. In addition, the patron, and in some cases the patron's heir, had claims on the freed slave's estate depending on its size and the number of children named as heirs in the freed slave's will. In effect, the ex-master's limited claim to the ex-slave's labor included the products of the ex-slave's labor after the laborer's death.

Freed slaves also suffered disabilities in public law that denied them access to the offices and ranks that conferred social prestige on members of Roman society. Freedmen, no matter how wealthy, were barred from the Roman senate and the offices and priesthoods held by the senatorial class. Freedmen and freedwomen could not marry a member of a senatorial family. Technically, freedmen could not enter the equestrian order, and, in most cities, their servile past disqualified them from the municipal offices and senate. They could not serve in the legions and, later, in the praetorian guard or urban cohorts. Further, the same vulnerability that freed slaves experienced in relations with their patrons characterized their relations with the state. Ex-slaves invariably received harsher punishments than the freeborn during political crises and, not even in principle, were they exempt from torture. When a patron was murdered, the freed slaves living under the same roof fared little better than the slaves who could be tortured and killed.

Freed slaves were not an economic class. Roman literature focuses on imperial freedmen who held high posts on the emperor's staff and wealthy freedmen who lacked good taste. Many more freed slaves, in fact, were craftsmen or shopkeepers, freed by craftsmen and shopkeepers, or they were the domestic servants of the social elite who continued to serve in the households of their former owners. Ex-slaves' relations with patrons, too, varied: some had close ties with their patrons, managed their property, worked in their shops, or married their former owners; others had no living patron, no obligations to the patron's heir, or were themselves the heirs of their former owners.

In different, albeit parallel, ways, legal status and social standing marked who made decisions and commanded obedience in Roman society and who obeyed. Magistrates commanded citizens; generals soldiers; parents children; masters slaves; patrons freed slaves. Each position of command meant not only power but also authority – the right to make decisions and demand obedience. In each position, a person was seen to take positive actions and to have duties. That is, power in these positions was legitimate and legal, although we must note that the Roman social and political elite defined what was legal and legitimate.

The arrangement of Roman society was very hierarchical. The roles of father and master were available to many male citizens. Mothers, too, claimed the respect and duty of children; as slaveholders, women commanded slaves. The rich and socially prominent looked down on their social inferiors. The roles of magistrate and general were available only to the upper classes, especially to men of the senatorial class. Yet any male Roman citizen was a privileged person in the Mediterranean after Rome's conquests. That experience was available to him because he was a legitimate member of the conquering state.

History and Slavery: Republic, Principate, and Empire

The political history that shaped this social order also shaped the history of slavery at Rome (Figure 18). A brief account of the history of the Roman Republic and the Principate, then, forms a useful framework for a narrower focus on the history of slavery. Republic and Principate signal different arrangements of power in the Roman state. In the Republic (509–27 BCE), although ordinary citizens had a political role, the senatorial class ruled Rome, Italy, and, by the second century BCE, an empire – territories governed directly by Rome as provinces and states or peoples controlled indirectly through various means. In the Principate, Rome, Italy, the empire, senators, and citizens were ruled by one man whom we call emperor and whom the Romans called *princeps*. Most important both for political developments and for the development of slavery was the growth of empire.

From early in its history, the Roman Republic was at war in Italy and then beyond. Roman victories resulted in Rome's control over the losers and a redirection of resources from conquered to conqueror. This expansion and its results belong to the development of empire. At first, Roman expansion was limited to Italy (Map 1). By the mid-third century BCE, all of Italy south of the Po River was under Roman control. Roman expansion outside of Italy began in the second half of the third century BCE with the First and Second Punic Wars, two wars against Carthage, a powerful state in North Africa with territories in Spain, Sicily, and Sardinia. Victory in 201 BCE brought Rome's first provinces and involvement in North Africa and Greece. Roman legions fought in these areas and in Asia Minor during the second century BCE, a century of nearly continuous war. At its end, Rome ruled all of the Mediterranean. The first century saw further war, conquests, and areas brought under Roman direct rule (Map 2).

Empire enlarged the power of the Roman senate and those who held office at Rome. It also meant an enormous increase in the wealth of Roman society, especially of the upper classes. Wealth came from plunder, taxes, payments imposed on the conquered by the Romans,

THE ROMAN SOCIAL ORDER AND A HISTORY OF SLAVERY

POLITICAL EVENTS	HISTORY OF SLAVERY
REPUBLIC (509–27 BCE)	

Early Republic (509–264 BCE)

POLITICAL EVENTS	HISTORY OF SLAVERY
• Struggle among different social groups (called the Struggle of the Orders) • 12 Tables (451/450 BCE) • Conquest or control of Italy south of the Po River • Samnite Wars (343–341, 326–305, 289–290 BCE)	• Legal distinction of status of slaves and freed slaves • Debt slavery • Abolition of debt slavery, 326 BCE • Enslavement of larger numbers of the conquered

Middle Republic (264–133 BCE)

• Punic Wars (264–241, 218–201, 149–146 BCE) • Conquest of overseas empire • Cato the Elder (consul 195, censor 184 BCE)	• Mass enslavements; increase of slaves in Italy • Beginning of increased slave labor in the countryside • Development of a "slave system"

Late Republic (133–127 BCE)

• Frequent periods of civil strife and struggle • Military dynasts: Marius, Sulla, Pompey, Caesar • Further conquests (esp. Gaul, 58–51 BCE) • Assassination of Caesar (44 BCE) • Octavian's Victory over Marc Antony (31 BCE)	• First Slave War (c. 135–132 BCE) • Second Slave War (c. 104–101 BCE) • Spartacus revolt (73–71 BCE) • Stories of slaves saving and betraying their owners • Clodius and Milo use slaves for political violence

PRINCIPATE (27 BCE–235 CE)	

POLITICAL EVENTS	HISTORY OF SLAVERY
Julio-Claudian Emperors (27 BCE–68 CE) • Augustus (27 BCE–14 CE) • Tiberius (14–37 CE) • Gaius (Caligula) (37–41 CE) • Claudius (41–54 CE) • Conquest of Britain • Nero (54–68 CE) • Jewish War (66–70 CE)	• Regulation of marriages to freed slaves, manumission, and status of freed slave • Tiberius to Marcus Aurelius: regulations on treatment of slaves and their status • Development of Stoic discourse of slavery
Civil War (68–69 CE)	• Development of Christianity
Flavian Emperors (69–96 CE) • Vespasian (69–79 CE) • Titus (79–81 CE) • Domitian (81– 96 CE) • Trajan (98–117 CE) • Dacian Wars (101–102, 105–106 CE) • Hadrian (117–138 CE)	• Late first–third centuries, decline of slave labor in the countryside
Antonine Emperors (138–193 CE) • Antoninus Pius (138–161 CE) • Marcus Aurelius (161–180 CE) • Commodus (178–193 CE)	
Severan Emperors (193–235 CE) • Caracalla (198–217 CE)	
Constantine (323 –337 CE)	

18. Roman political history and slavery. All emperors from 27 BCE to 193 CE are listed; thereafter, only those mentioned by name in a chapter. The events of Roman political history and the history of Roman slavery do not line up exactly.

and extortion. Those who benefited most were generals, senatorial governors, and the *publicani* (equestrian tax collectors). Those enriched displayed their wealth, and that display distinguished them. The elite spent their wealth in the public arena, giving elaborate games or building temples, monuments, roads, drains, and aqueducts. Some supported poorer men with private largesse. Marcus Licinius Crassus, reputed to be the wealthiest man in first-century Rome, for example, gave daily dinners at his home for anyone and everyone. Above all, Rome's upper classes began to live like the rulers of empire they were. Their elaborate houses, fancy possessions, servants, and costly interest in art and culture reflected their power.

In the last century BCE, empire shaped a series of social and political conflicts at Rome. The power struggles that had always characterized the Roman oligarchy became more destructive, flaring into civil wars fought in Rome, Italy, and throughout the Mediterranean. A series of powerful and at times nearly independent generals whom historians call military dynasts – Marius, Sulla, Pompey, and Julius Caesar – won great victories outside Rome and then used their armies to settle their political conflicts at home. The wars split the ruling class and set citizen against citizen across the battlefield. Each time, the end of one of these struggles meant confiscation of the property of the losers, along with proscriptions – lists of those who could be killed for a bounty. The last of these struggles pitted Julius Caesar's chief lieutenant, Marc Antony, against Caesar's adopted son, Octavian.

After his victory over Antony, Octavian, who in 27 BCE took the name Augustus, settled the political situation at Rome, founding the Principate (Figures 19a and b). Members of his extended family followed him as emperor, until a civil war in 69–70 CE brought a change of ruling families, followed later by emperors from other families or the military. In effect, the Principate was a military dictatorship dressed in republican form by its founder. Many of the institutions of the Republic continued: the senate met and magistrates were elected. Effective power, especially control of the legions and

19. (a) Augustus as conqueror, Rome, early first century CE. (Alinari/Art Resource, New York. Braccio Nuovo, Museo Chiaramonti, Vatican Museums, Vatican State) (b) Augustus as *pontifex maximus* (head of the state religion), Rome, after 12 BCE. (Erich Lessing/Art Resource, New York)

provinces, however, was in the hands of the *princeps*. The emperor's power expanded and with it an imperial administration, staffed originally by the emperor's own slaves and freedmen, until in the late first century CE the top posts were taken by equestrians. It took nearly a century of struggle with the *princeps* for the former ruling class to find its political place in the new order as civil servants. When, in the first century, the emperor Caligula announced, "I can treat anyone exactly as I please," the sentiment was thoroughly objectionable to the senate. By the second century CE, however, the maxim of law was "the will of the prince has the force of law," and all, including the senatorial class, accepted this equation.

The shape and character of the state changed: by the second century CE, we can talk about something we might call a world state or an imperial state. In the mid-second century, the orator Aelius Aristides imagined the empire as "one continuous country and one people" under the rule of its "director in chief," the emperor. This conception is a long way from the Roman empire at the end of the Republic, when the city of Rome dominated Italy and the provinces, senators came from Rome and Italy, and few outside of Italy were Roman citizens. Over the course of the Principate, citizenship and membership in the senatorial order, the elite of empire, were extended to those who adopted Greco-Roman cultural and political forms. By the second century CE, citizens and senators came from all over the empire. In 212 CE the emperor Caracalla granted Roman citizenship to all free residents of the empire who did not yet have it; what had been membership in a city-state was extended to the world. By then, however, wealth, not citizenship, guaranteed legal privilege, and by the time all free residents of the empire were citizens, all, rich and poor, had become subjects of the emperor. In addition, Mediterranean forms of life – classical city-state political forms, Latin and Greek languages, Roman entertainments and architecture – spread from the coast inland and were found throughout this world.

In the third century, barbarian invasions, war on all the frontiers of the empire, and political instability created a crisis whose solution changed the Roman world: by the late third century, the empire had an elaborate bureaucracy devoted to extracting resources for the army; increased taxation burdened subjects and citizens; and military men dominated the governance of empire. In 312 CE the conversion of the emperor Constantine to Christianity stimulated widespread conversion among the ruling classes, and the Christianization of the empire reshaped society and cultural norms (Figure 20). A fourth-century aristocrat on his estate could imagine that he was still living in the world of the second century CE, but, in fact, the world of the Roman Empire had changed irrevocably.

20. Head of Constantine, Rome,
c. 315–330 CE. (Sansani, Neg. D-DAI
Rom 1957.0998)

Setting a history of slavery at Rome within this political chronology highlights other aspects of the growth of empire and an imperial
state and, at points, introduces new concerns. Like the history of the
Roman state, the history of Roman slavery was not static; a large-scale
slave society emerged with and within empire, faced a violent challenge in the slave rebellions of the late second and early first centuries
BCE, stabilized, and, finally, began to change fundamentally in the
late first century CE. A fuller discussion of these developments below
recounts the history of the institution of slavery rather than the history
of individual slaves, so, in effect, it is a masters' narrative, although this
narrative shaped the conditions in which individual slaves lived. In the
period of the great slave rebellions (c. 135–70 BCE), however, individual slaves emerge in this masters' narrative as historical agents on a
par with Roman generals and politicians.

Although there were slaves in early Roman society, early Rome
cannot be called a slave society in the sense defined in Chapter 1 – a
society in which slaves exist in significantly large numbers and produce
the bulk of the income of the rich. It appears that citizen debt bondsmen, rather than slaves, provided dependent labor for the wealthy.

Debt slavery was not a matter of lending money and collecting interest but a means of claiming the labor of the poor. The loan in the form of subsistence or grain was secured on the person of the debtor (or his son) for the very purpose of controlling the labor of the debtor.

By the fifth century BCE, slave and free, however, were distinguished in law. The Twelve Tables (451–450 BCE), the earliest Roman law, sets out harsher punishment for the slave thief than the free thief, and compensation for an injury to a free person was higher than compensation for injuring a slave. Slaves could be sold in Rome itself, and they were distinguished from citizen debt bondsmen, who could be sold into slavery only across the Tiber (i.e., outside the ancient boundary of Rome). The regulation marked the slave as outsider even before conquests outside Italy brought foreign slaves to Rome.

Despite the legal distinction between slave and free, debt bondage and harsh treatment by magistrates and powerful men limited the citizenship of the poor and the powerless, narrowing in practice the distance between free and slave. From the fifth through the early third centuries BCE, poorer citizens continuously agitated for protection against the summary treatment of officials and the powerful, for debt relief, and finally for the abolition of debt bondage. By the end of their struggle, protection, the right of appeal against the actions of officials, and the abolition of debt bondage (326 BCE) firmly divided slave from citizen and defined the physical integrity of the citizen against the vulnerability of the slave.

Mass enslavement in Rome's foreign wars made possible the growth of a large-scale slave system. First, war increased the slave population in Italy and continually fed that population with new captives. Rome's early wars in Italy had resulted in the enslavement of some of the conquered, but the enslavement of large numbers of the conquered apparently began with Rome's wars with the Samnites, a people in south central Italy (343–341, 327–321, 316–304, 298–290 BCE) – in other words, around the time that the elite was losing citizens as its primary source of dependent labor. The Roman conquest of the Mediterranean in the second century BCE escalated the numbers of slaves. Roman

21. Head of Gaius Julius Caesar, Turin, c. 44 BCE. (Koppermann, Neg. D-DAI-Rom 1974.1565)

victories meant major dislocations of people, primarily importation to Italy.

The Roman sources are relentless and matter of fact in their notices of 1,000 captives sold here, 5,000 there, the population of this tribe enslaved, the inhabitants of that city captured and sold. Although the numbers given in ancient sources are notoriously unreliable, a few examples indicate the scale of capture and enslavement. In 177 BCE during his campaign in Sardinia, Tiberius Sempronius Gracchus killed or enslaved 80,000 of the island's inhabitants (Livy 41.28.9). So many captives flooded the slave market that this glut of human property produced the Roman saying "Sardinians for sale, one more worthless than the next" (Festus 428). In 167 BCE the senate granted the victorious Roman general in Greece the right to sack seventy cities in Epirus (on the west coast of Greece): 150,000 persons were enslaved (Livy 45.34.5). In 57 BCE Julius Caesar sold 53,000 of the Aduatuci into slavery (Caesar, *Gallic War* 2.33), and the total number of captives of Caesar's Gallic campaigns between 58 and 51 BCE has been put at one million (Appian, *Gallic History* 1.2) (Figure 21). The Romans did not always enslave the conquered, but conquest remained the most important source of slaves in the Republic, adding to the numbers of people enslaved in other ways: piracy, the slave trade, birth, and children abandoned or sold by impoverished parents. As noted in Chapter 1, estimates of the size of the slave population vary. By the late first century BCE, probably 20–30 percent of the population of Roman Italy were slaves – 1 to 1.5 million out of a population of 5 to 6 million.

Second, Rome's conquest of the Mediterranean altered agricultural production in Italy in a way that shaped a large-scale slave system economically over a period of two centuries. Although it has been challenged in recent years, the dominant view of historians emphasizes the increasing importance of slavery in the Italian countryside. Free peasants continued to farm land, but slaves, not citizen debt bondsmen, produced the income of the rich on landholdings enlarged by the effects of empire. Rome's wars drew free peasants off the land into the armies, and their victories resulted in the flow of slaves discussed above. The elite, enriched by the wealth of empire, put together extensive holdings, farmed by the slaves won in Rome's wars. Slaves could be exploited in a way free citizen peasantry could not be, and there was no danger this labor force would be drawn off the land into the legions. In addition, in the cities, as the elite devoted the wealth of empire to elaborate houses and goods, many slaves served in the households of the wealthy as domestic servants, shaping what came to be seen as the appropriate lifestyle of elite men and women – living nobly.

How to use and to manage slaves, especially in agricultural production for the market, became concerns for the large landowner. In other words, empire and its effects on the Roman economy raised questions about slavery as an institution. How were slaves to be organized? What behavior did slaveholders expect and need for production? What sort of treatment enabled that behavior? A system of practices and ideas that maintained a slave system, however, did not arise in one moment or all at once. The practices of the republican statesman and author Cato the Elder (234–149 BCE) and his manual on farming show us the mixed beginning of a system of the methodical organization, control, and use of human property, or at least the perceived need for it. At the same time, Cato's treatment of slaves indicates a brutal disregard for their lives.

Cato's own practices and his written advice aimed to make farming a profitable enterprise, and this goal shaped his treatment of slaves. Utility determined the acquisition of new slaves and the disposal of old ones. Cato bought new captives because he thought they were trainable, like puppies or foals (Plutarch, *Life of Cato* 21.1), and he advised the landholder to sell off old and sick slaves, just as he should sell off oxen, cattle, sheep, old carts, or tools that were not up to standard or unneeded (*On Agriculture* 2.7). To extract the most labor from his slaves, the slaveholder should calculate the tasks to be done and the time they should take, counsels Cato (*On Agriculture* 2.2). Slaves should be employed in indoor tasks when bad weather prohibited work in the field or vineyard (*On Agriculture* 2.3). Again, to ensure the labor of workers, they should be provided with adequate provisions of food, wine, oil, and clothing (*On Agriculture* 56–59).

Control loomed large in Cato's concerns. He wanted slaves to be either at work or asleep: at work they were busy, asleep "easier to control." He encouraged dissention among his slaves, fearing moments when the group of slaves was in agreement. For serious offenses, he tried the offender before all of the slaves and killed him if found guilty – a practice that inculcated proper servile behavior and displayed the consequence of bad conduct (Plutarch, *Life of Cato* 21.2–4). Some worked in chains (*On Agriculture* 56) and, we know from other sources, were housed in *ergastula* (slave prisons). The overseer (called a *vilicus,* himself a slave) managed the slave workers in the absence of the slaveholder, and Cato provides detailed instructions for the owner's control of the *vilicus* and for the *vilicus's* control of the slaves (*On Agriculture* 5; see Chapter 5).

Other slaveholders were apparently less systematic or less concerned with the basic needs of their human property. At least, brutality and a lack of control were cited as the conditions leading to the first major slave rebellion in c. 135 BCE:

> Almost everyone as he got richer adopted first a luxurious, and then an arrogant and provocative pattern of behaviour. As a result of these developments, slaves were coming to be treated worse and worse, and were correspondingly more and more alienated from their owners. ... All men who owned a lot of land bought up entire consignments of slaves to work their farms ... some were bound with chains, some were worn out by the hard work they were given to do; they branded all of them with humiliating brand-marks. ... The Sicilians who controlled all this wealth were competing in arrogance, greed, and injustice with the Italians. Those Italians who owned a lot of slaves had accustomed their herdsmen to irresponsible behaviour to such an extent that instead of providing them with rations they encouraged them to rob. (Diodorus Siculus 34.2.26–27, trans. T. Wiedemann)

For the historian Diodorus Siculus, the development of large-scale slavery accompanied by the abusive treatment of slaves, the failure to provide for their basic needs, and a lack of control led to disastrous results.

In the late second and early first centuries BCE, Italy and Sicily experienced the only mass slave rebellions in Roman history. Since these larger rebellions were preceded by smaller, less extensive slave revolts, the rebellions represent a larger phenomenon and challenge to the emerging slave society at Rome. Although told from a Roman point of view long after the rebellions, the stories of these rebellions show the effects of the precipitous rise of the slave population, continually replenished by new captives; the beginnings of a system of control, not fully articulated or even practiced; and the potential brutality of every slaveholder within a conquest mentality. The stories also indicate the potential contradictions between the conquests that won empire and the rules that governed those already under Roman control.

The first two rebellions, the First and Second Slave Wars (c. 135–132 and c. 104–101 BCE), took place in Sicily, Rome's first province, where, after the second war with Carthage, wealthy Romans and Italians had bought up large holdings and used slave labor for the production of grain and stock raising. The First Slave War, recounted by Diodorus Siculus, began with a rising against a particularly brutal master named Damophilos, a citizen of Enna, a city in the center of Sicily (Map 3). His slaves consulted a slave from another household, a Syrian named Eunous, a magician and a wonder worker who could foresee the future. On his advice, they broke open the slave prisons and with a force of 400 slaves attacked the residents of the city. Afterward, they met in the theater, put Damophilos and his equally cruel wife on trial (he was killed before it could be completed), and chose Eunous as king. The rebels moved into the surrounding countryside, attracting other slaves who increased the number of rebels to 6,000. About a month later, in the south of the island, Kleon, a slave from Cilicia and a horse breeder, led another slave revolt. With a force of 5,000 fellow slaves, he took the city of Agrigentum. Eunous and Kleon joined forces and defeated the Roman army sent against them. The Roman estimates of the total number of slaves involved in the rebellion range from 60,000 to 200,000. After several years of campaigns of varying success, the Romans finally quelled the rebellion in 132 BCE by recovering Taormina and Enna, two key centers of resistance. Kleon was killed, and Eunous captured. The senate sent a commission to settle the political situation in the province, but the extensive use of slaves continued, as did the influx of slaves from Rome's wars. Although the Roman commander supposedly had wiped out all traces of the rebellion, less than thirty years later (c. 104 BCE), thousands of slaves again rose in revolt against their owners.

The story of the Second Slave War, as told by Diodorus Siculus, begins with another problem of large-scale slavery and empire: who can be enslaved and who cannot (Map 3). During a war in northern Italy against a German tribe called the Cimbri, the senate allowed the Roman commander to call for help from Rome's overseas allies. When

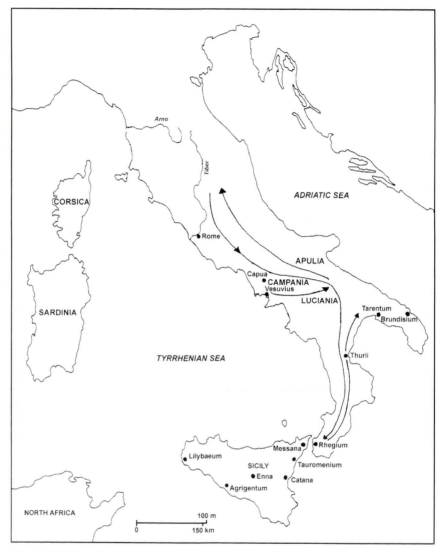

Map 3. Sicilian Slave Wars and the Spartacus Revolt. (Reproduced from *The Archaeology of Greek and Roman Slavery*, p. 256, fig. 106, courtesy of the Society of Antiquaries of London, © 2003, reserved)

the king of Bithynia, a kingdom in what is now northwest Turkey, received the request, he claimed that he had no one to send because the Roman tax collectors had seized many Bithynians and enslaved them in other territories of the Roman empire. The senate passed a decree that "no free ally should serve as a slave in the Roman empire and that Roman governors should see to it that these persons be set free" (36.3.2). The Roman governor of Sicily began hearing petitions from slaves, and more than 800 slaves were freed in a few days. Other slaves' hopes of freedom, however, were squelched by the wealthy land- and slaveholders in the province:

> Everyone who was in slavery anywhere on the island was ecstatic at the hope of regaining their freedom. But the people who mattered got together and appealed to the governor not to carry his intentions into effect. Perhaps he was persuaded by money, or else had no freedom of action because of the favours they had done him; he abandoned his keenness to pass judgment in these cases, turned away those who came to him to get back their freedom and told them to go back to their own particular owners. (Diodorus Siculus 36.3.2–3, trans. T. Wiedemann)

The remaining slaves who had gathered in Syracuse to petition for their freedom left the city and fled to the shrine of the Palikoi (a traditional place of asylum for slaves escaping brutal masters), where they considered revolt. Slave risings followed in other parts of Sicily. Two hundred slaves attacked local landowners at Halikyai, although the governor put down the revolt. Another rising of eighty slaves escalated to 2,000 slaves. They defeated the Roman forces sent against them, and their numbers tripled. They chose a slave named Salvius as their king. Like the leaders of the First Slave War, he, too, had a religious or miraculous aura: "he was thought to know all about divination and played ecstatic music on the flute at festivals for women" (Diodorus Siculus 36.4.4). He organized the slave forces, now over 20,000, and attacked the city of Morgantina, although without success. Another revolt in western Sicily was led by Athenion, a Cilician slave, who was a slave overseer and a talented astrologer. Athenion freed the slaves in the slave prisons: the number of slaves in revolt grew from about 1,000 to 10,000. He, too, was chosen king. After a struggle between the two slave leaders, they joined forces to face the Roman army sent against them. Fighting continued until 101 BCE when the Romans defeated the slaves, killing Athenion and capturing a group of 1,000 rebel slaves led by a man named Satyrus. They were sent to Rome and condemned to fight wild animals in the arena. Rather than suffering a humiliating death as a spectacle for the Romans, "they ended their lives in a particularly glorious way; instead of fighting the animals, they killed each other at the public altars, and Satyrus himself killed the last man, and then heroically committed suicide after all the others" (Diodorus Siculus 36.10.3).

A generation later, slaves in the heartland of empire revolted. This rebellion bears the name of its leader, Spartacus (Map 3). Well known in European and American literature long before the 1960 Stanley Kubrick film starring Kirk Douglas, the slave gladiator Spartacus was counted among Rome's great enemies by the late first century BCE, and his very name became synonymous with the dangers posed by slaves. The revolt began in a gladiatorial school in Capua, a city that had seen two slave revolts in the late second century BCE. Gladiator combats, known but not widespread, were just becoming a common and very popular entertainment at Rome, and Capua was a major center for the training of gladiators. Seventy slave gladiators, including Gauls, Germans, and Thracians, many of them recently enslaved, used kitchen tools to break out of the gladiatorial school. They seized a wagonload of gladiatorial arms and established a base on Mount Vesuvius from which they raided the countryside. The rebels attracted slaves from the neighboring villas, increasing their numbers. Twice, they defeated the Roman forces sent against them. From Roman accounts of the rebellions, it is difficult to determine whether Spartacus led his forces, following a strategic plan that the Romans never quite divined, or simply reacted to the conflicting opinions among the slaves themselves. First, the slaves, whose numbers had escalated to 70,000, moved south into Lucania and Apulia. Next, they turned north, perhaps with the intention of escaping Italy and returning to their homes. They defeated a Roman army and again turned south, at one point threatening the city of Rome itself. At the end of 72 BCE both consuls, with Marcus Licinius Crassus at the head of the army of ten legions, were deployed against Spartacus's army. Crassus drove Spartacus and his followers toward Rhegium. The slaves may have planned to cross into Sicily, the site of the two earlier rebellions, but they remained in Bruttium, besieged by Crassus. In 71 BCE the slave army tried to break out to reach the port of Brundisium on the east coast of Italy, but when they received news of a Roman army returning from the East, they faced Crassus in a pitched battle. The slaves were defeated, Spartacus was killed, and 6,000 of the defeated slaves were crucified along the Via Appia from Capua to Rome. Since the road was 211 kilometers long, anyone traveling between Rome and Capua encountered a crucified slave every thirty-five meters or so. The spectacle served as a brutal warning of the fate of slave rebels and a memorable display of the futility of rebellion.

Although there were smaller-scale, local revolts after 70 BCE, the defeat of Spartacus ended the era of rebellions involving thousands of slaves. Why this was so, and why these revolts failed, are difficult questions to answer. It seems that the slave system stabilized, and perhaps the 6,000 crucifixions did their work among the slave population, discouraging similar revolts. Then, too, we must acknowledge the difficulty of such large-scale rebellions for the slaves themselves and their leaders. Holding together and organizing thousands of slaves of different origins and languages was a formidable task. The slave rebels may have tried to solidify, if not maintain, a freedom won by violence. In the view of some scholars, slaves in the three great slave rebellions between 135 and 70 BCE used kingship, the charisma or religious aura of slave leaders, military organization, and the control of food and weapons to organize themselves in a paramilitary fashion in defended locations to establish lives outside of slavery. Ultimately, as we have seen, these practices failed. In the end, the slave rebels could not withstand the armed force of the Roman state.

However inaccurate the Roman stories recounted long after the rebellions, it seems clear that they began as local revolts, not planned large-scale uprisings, and escalated spontaneously: each local revolt gathered followers from slaves on estates and slave herdsmen who already led lives on the edge of brigandage. This aspect of the rebellions, however, indicates widespread discontent among slaves and a willingness to deal with the brutality of their condition by rejecting servitude in open and violent revolt. By 73 BCE, after the failure of the two great Sicilian rebellions, slaves who joined Spartacus must have been brave, desperate, or both. Even if the Roman sources exaggerate the numbers of slave rebels, the history of Roman slavery, nonetheless, would include thousands of people throwing off their enslavement in a series of revolts that covered large territories in Sicily and Italy. The dimensions of all three revolts suggest the lack of systematic means of control and organization of slave labor, especially of a population replenished by captives recently reduced to bondage. The circumstances that precipitated the Second Slave War, too, indicate that empire and the Roman conquest of the Mediterranean had created tensions, if not contradictions, in the distinction between ruled and enslaved, and we must suspect that slave rebellions that included such large numbers of newly enslaved captives had elements of a provincial revolt, albeit of provincials in the heartland of empire.

Although there were no more large-scale slave rebellions, the Romans constantly feared slave revolts. The truism of Roman slaveholders was *tot servi, quot hostes* – you have as many enemies as you have slaves. In the civil struggles of the last century BCE, Roman politicians claimed that their opponents freed slaves who then joined their liberators' struggles with their own political adversaries. In fact, some Roman politicians used their slaves in conflicts with other politicians. Most famously, two politicians of the 50s BCE, Clodius and Milo, deployed armed slaves in their struggles with other politicians and each other. Beyond the use of armed slaves in the violent struggles of free men, the social disorder and civil wars of the last century BCE filled Roman slave owners with an apprehension of a world turned upside down in which slaves could easily betray their owners. Moreover, in this topsy-turvy world, as a sign of disorder, came charges that too many slaveholders freed their slaves for the wrong reasons, polluting the citizen body with the unworthy: some slaves were freed as a reward because they had abetted their masters in "poisonings, murders, and crimes against the gods or community" and others for frivolous reasons or for the popularity that would accrue to the master, claims Dionysius of Halicarnassus, a teacher of rhetoric in the late first century BCE (*History of Rome* 4.24.5). Other authors add that some freed slaves made their fortunes in the proscriptions that cost the social elite their lives, civil status, and property: as Pliny the Elder puts its, freed slaves who once stood on the auctioneer's platform "gained wealth at the expense of the Roman citizens' blood in the license that resulted from the pro-scriptions" (*Natural History* 35.200).

Augustus's victory in his struggle with Marc Antony and his establishment of the Principate ended the civil wars. The end of the Republic's continuous wars of expansion and the restoration of social order had repercussions for the institution of slavery. The political change from Republic to Principate raises questions about the supply of slaves in the Principate. The standard view has it that the wars of conquest in the middle and late Republic brought plenty of slaves to Italy at a cheap price. Some historians have assumed that captives were primarily men, so natural reproduction played little role as a source of slaves. After the closing down of extensive military campaigns in the early Principate, they argue, the number of female slaves increased and natural reproduction became the more important source of slaves.

There are two problems with this view. First, accounts of Roman conquests in the Republic depict the enslavement of women and chil-dren. The assumed absence of slave women and their increased num-bers in the Principate may have more to do with our sources than with reality: the sources pay more attention to home-born slaves and

22. Relief of Claudius's conquest of Britain, Aphrodisias, mid-first century CE. This relief comes from a monument celebrating the emperors from Augustus to Nero. Claudius is nude (a sign of his heroic status) but for a helmet and flowing mantle; Britain is depicted as a prostrate woman. The emperor pins her down and pulls her by her hair. (Photo M. Ali Dögenci, Courtesy of New York University Excavations at Aphrodisias)

the reproduction of female slaves in the last years of the Republic and in the Principate. In different but parallel ways, the historians Keith Bradley and Ulrike Roth both argue compellingly that slave women were present in the countryside from an early period in the development of the slave system at Rome (Bradley 1994; Roth 2007). Second, although the nearly continuous wars of expansion of the last two centuries BCE came to an end, Rome still waged wars and enslaved many of the conquered. To name a few, Augustus's wars against the Alpine tribes and in Spain, Tiberius's wars along the Rhine, Claudius's conquest of Britain (Figure 22), campaigns against the Parthians, Trajan's wars in Dacia (Figures 25–26, 29, 31), and Marcus Aurelius's campaign across the Danube all brought captives to Rome as slaves. Revolts in the provinces, although more rare (or underreported), also resulted in enslavements. In the Jewish War in 66–70 CE, to take a dramatic

23. (a) Arch of Titus, Rome, after 81 CE. (Schwanke, Neg. D–DAI–Rom 1979.2000) (b) Relief of the spoils from Jerusalem, Arch of Titus, Rome, after 81 CE. (Sansani, Neg. D–DAI Rom 1957.0893)

example, 97,000 people were enslaved (Figures 23a and b). Thus, war captives continued to supply Rome with slaves and must be counted as a source of slaves along with children born into slavery, abandoned infants raised as slaves, and men and women brought into the empire in the long-distance slave trade.

Moreover, as they had in the Republic, enslaved captives figured in the triumphal celebrations and monuments of the emperors (Figure 23b). Titus, the son of the emperor Vespasian, for example, sent

24. From the triumphal frieze on the Temple of Apollo Sosianus, Rome, c. 20 CE. (Singer, Neg. D-DAI Rom 1971.0045)

700 captives from the Jewish War to parade in his father's and his own triumph (71 CE): in the procession the captives marched amid the gold, silver, and ivory objects seized as plunder, animals, and representations of the Roman destruction. The last included scenes of people fleeing the Romans and people led into captivity, so the procession celebrating the military glory of the emperor and his son displayed both images of the enslaved enemy and the newly enslaved themselves – clothed in elaborate garments that hid the scars and wounds of war.

Live spectacles of captives were fixed in stone on monuments like the Temple of Apollo Sosianus built under Augustus and Trajan's Column in Rome. Part of the decorative frieze on the Temple of Apollo included a triumphal procession. In one fragment, attendants begin to lift a platform that holds a trophy, a pole hung with arms; two defeated captives chained to the trophy complete the scenario (Figure 24). The story of Trajan's wars in Dacia (101–102, 105–106 CE) depicted on the emperor's column unfolds in stock scenes that include subjected Dacians. Captives show up repeatedly in these reliefs. In one scene, for example, a soldier grabs a Dacian prisoner by the hair and pushes him

25. Dacian brought before Trajan on Trajan's Column, Rome, 113 CE. (su concessione del Minstero per i Beni e le Attività Culturali – Soprintendenza Speciale per i Beni Archeologici di Roma)

toward Trajan (Figure 25). In another, defeated Dacians kneel at the feet of the victorious emperor, while others stand nearby with their hands bound behind their backs (Figure 26).

The Principate brought other changes to the slave system at Rome: most importantly, the regulation of both manumission and the relations of owner and slave. In effect, the state took control of certain actions and treatments that had been totally in the hands of individual masters and patrons in the Republic. Augustus's political changes were accompanied by a reordering of society. The latter included laws on the number of slaves an owner could manumit in his will and the conditions of manumission. Augustus's law set the legal age of manumission at thirty, providing stipulations for special circumstances. His marriage laws forbade marriages between freed slaves and senators, senator's children, grandchildren, and great-grandchildren, although

26. Dacians surrender to Trajan on Trajan's Column, Rome, 113 CE. (su concessione del Minstero per i Beni e le Attività Culturali – Soprintendenza Speciale per i Beni Archeologici di Roma)

the laws were unconcerned with marriages between ordinary citizens and freed slaves. He allowed freedmen to serve in the fleet (often as commanders) and the *vigiles* (the fire brigades in Rome). Barred from the Roman magistracies and municipal offices, successful freedmen found recognition in membership in the *Augustales,* boards of freedmen dedicated to worship of the emperor and public improvements in their cities. More modest but propertied freedmen could serve as *vicomagistri,* officials of the 265 *vici* (wards) into which Augustus divided the city: these officials regulated traffic, watched out for crime and fires in their districts, and sacrificed to the Lares of the Crossroads and the *genius* (spirit) of the emperor. On the Altar of the Vicomagistri of the Vicus Aesculeti, these officials stand on two sides of the altar: they wear togas, the formal dress of Roman male citizens; their heads are covered for the sacrifice; their outstretched hands hold the implements for the rite (Figure 27).

27. Relief from Altar of Vicomagistri of the Vicus Aesculeti, Rome, 2 CE. (Photo Michael Larvey su concessione del Minstero per i Beni e le Attività Culturali – Soprintendenza Speciale per i Beni Archeologici di Roma)

Later emperors regulated the treatment of slaves. Claudius ordered that sick slaves abandoned by their masters on the island of Aesculapius were free if they recovered. Another law passed before 79 CE prohibited masters from condemning their slaves to fight wild beasts in the arena unless they proved the cause for this punishment before the appropriate magistrate. Domitian banned the castration of slaves for commercial purposes, and several emperors limited the prostitution of female slaves, in particular, those whose terms of sale forbade their use as prostitutes. Hadrian regulated excessive severity in individual cases, prohibited the use of slave prisons (*ergastula*), and forbade the sale of individuals to pimps and gladiatorial trainers and suppliers unless cause was shown for such treatment. Antoninus Pius made slaveholders liable for homicide if they killed their own slave without cause, just as they were if they killed another person's slave. He ordered that slaves who fled cruel treatment and sought refuge at a shrine or statue of the emperor were to be sold to a new owner if the original owner's treatment was judged to be unbearable.

Some scholars have seen in these measures a humanitarian concern for slaves. But, regardless of the benevolent attitudes of individual emperors, imperial legislation did not fundamentally change key aspects of the institution of slavery itself, especially the domination of owner over slave and the physical vulnerability of the slave. Imperial rulings limited excessive cruelty in the corporal punishment of slaves and their sexual use; however, they did not erase owners' physical domination of their slaves, nor did they interfere with owners' sexual relations with their own slaves. The state simply assumed a role in regulating an owner's domination. In many instances, certain punishments were not entirely forbidden but forbidden only without adequate cause. Cause was assessed by judges and officials who were themselves slaveholders and whose class bias favored the wealthy and socially prominent who were the largest slaveholders. Moreover, for the jurist Gaius, the central concern of such measures was not to improve the condition of slaves but to curb abuse in the right to administer property (1.53).

Some scholars, too, have observed the development of a humanitarian concern for slaves during the Principate in Stoicism, a philosophy taken up by some members of the elite, and Christianity, both of which acknowledged the humanity of slaves. The Stoic sought to live according to nature: every man, free or slave, had reason and was able to live in harmony with the rational principle that infuses the universe. Free or slave could live the virtuous life. However, the Stoics were more concerned with the inner life of individuals than their social condition: the freedom that counted was spiritual. For the Stoic, slavery, like other conditions, was an external circumstance to be endured. Any man could become a slave: fortune could turn the great man into a humble shepherd, the free man into a slave. Then, too, what man is not a slave, asked Seneca, Stoic writer, politician, and tutor of the emperor

Nero: "one man is a slave to lust, another to avarice, another to ambition, and all men are slaves to fear" (*Letters* 47.17). It is difficult to see how these views translated into practice. Men like the sympathetic Seneca did not turn their understanding of the humiliation of slavery into a call for manumission. Stoics advocated good treatment of slaves, which may have had effects in individual cases; however, kind masterly behavior and restraint were urged to improve the spiritual state of the master, not the social life of the slave.

Where Stoics addressed other members of the elite, Christians spoke to a wider audience, including quite directly the slaves themselves. "Slaves, be obedient to those who are your earthly masters, with fear and trembling, in singleness of heart, as to Christ; not in the way of eye-service, as men-pleasers, but as slaves of Christ doing the will of God from the heart, rendering service with a good will as to the Lord and not to men, knowing that whatever good any one does, he will receive the same again from the Lord, whether he is slave or free," says St. Paul in his Letter to the Ephesians (6.5). Christians considered slaves and free people equal before God, but their equality was spiritual and a matter of the rewards or punishments to come in the eternal life. Meanwhile, in this life the slave should obey his master, as a wife her husband, children their father, and every human God. More than this injunction to obedience, Christian theology made the patriarchal household with the *paterfamilias* holding power over wife, children, and slaves a working model for Christians' relations with God. On the level of practice, Christianity brought no changes to the Roman slave system, whatever other changes it introduced in social customs. Christians had slaves and showed the same concern as pagan slaveholders in the control and management of their slaves.

Rather than introducing a humanitarian concern for slaves, Stoicism and Christianity might be seen in terms of a masterly concern with the management of slaves. This development does not quite follow the chronology of Roman political history. We glimpse its beginning in the work of Cato the Elder and, later, in the letters of Cicero; however, a different, more systematic, or perhaps simply more articulated and self-conscious concern with masterly control and behavior appears in the late first century BCE in the agricultural manual of Varro, in the first century CE in the agricultural manual of Columella and the writings of Seneca, and in late first and early second centuries CE in the works of the politician and orator Pliny the Younger. Chapter 4 explores the two aspects of this concern: a management that reaches into the "psychology" of the slave and a benevolent paternalism that makes the treatment of slaves a feature of elite self-fashioning.

By the fifth century CE, the Roman slave society had changed. Slaves were no longer the dominant labor force on large estates in the countryside in Italy and Sicily, the traditional center of the Roman empire. Instead, the farms of the wealthy tended to be worked by peasants tied to the land. Historians no longer locate this change in the great transformation of Roman society that began in the economic and social crises of the third century CE. Nor do they view the development as a linear process in which slaves were replaced by bound peasants (*coloni*) who were the precursors of medieval serfs. The villa system of large estates farmed by slave labor that emerged in the wake of Roman imperialism spread to Gaul, Britain, Spain, and Africa, but it developed its own forms that relied on local types of dependent labor, not necessarily chattel slavery. In effect, slavery was not the dominant labor force in the empire from the end of the third century BCE to 200 CE, except in Italy and Sicily. Moreover, in this heartland, slave, free, and laborers tied by formal contract and patronage had all worked the land, but by the second century CE the decisive shift away from predominantly slave labor had begun in Italy itself. This is not to say slavery disappeared from the economy or society. There were still large numbers of slaves in late antiquity, serving primarily as domestic servants, agents, and administrators; the elite continued to distinguish themselves by a host of such slaves; and master–slave relations continued to figure importantly in both literature and law.

The following chapters, which look at the sale of slaves, the attitudes of Roman slaveholders, the material conditions of slaves, and their work, trace the violence that lay at the heart of slavery and the extreme inequality of power that characterized owner-slave relations; they also examine the ways that slaves could and did deal with their condition. Considerations of the violence and inequity of Roman slavery must take account of two themes that run through this chapter. First, Roman slavery existed in a society of unequal social relations in general, roughly defined by the poles of slave and free, poor and rich, lowly free citizens and the elite, and from 27 BCE on, subjects and emperors. Throughout the history of this society, the elite exploited their social inferiors – for example, as soldiers who fought Rome's wars and as tenants and occasional laborers. Second, violence characterized Roman history – riots, civil wars, slave rebellions, provincial revolts, and above all foreign wars. For long years in the Republic, Romans were inured to wars waged throughout the Mediterranean and beyond, and during periods in the Principate, Roman armies fought to maintain and extend the boundaries of empire – wars that brought captives to Italy and Rome. Perhaps, equally important, the Romans celebrated war, conquest, and the subjection of the defeated in rituals, monuments, public celebrations, and entertainments.

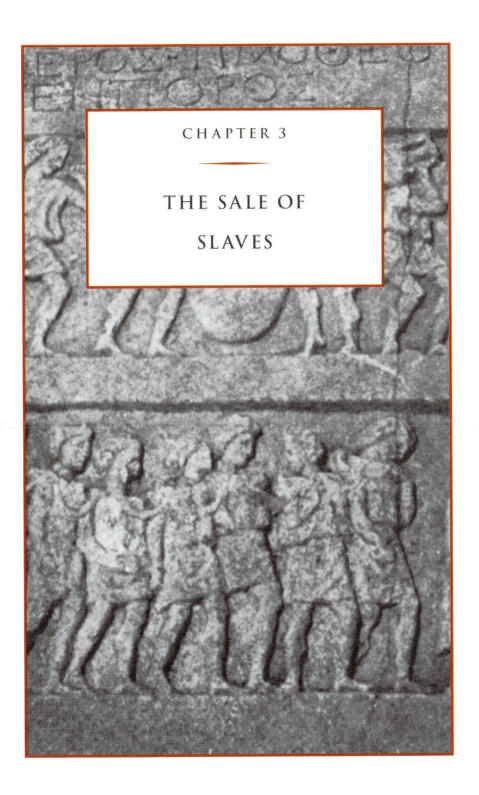

CHAPTER 3

THE SALE OF

SLAVES

Gaius Fabullius Macer, subaltern of the trireme "Tigris" of the praetorian fleet of Misenum, purchased from Quintus Julius Priscus, soldier of the same trireme in the same fleet, a boy of trans-Euphrates origin named Abbas, also known as Eutyches or by whatever other name he is called, about seven years old at a price of 200 denarii and the customs duty per head. Fabullius Macer demanded the formal acknowledgement in accordance with the edict that the boy was in good health. (*Fontes Iuris Romani Antejustiniani* 3.132, trans. N. Lewis and M. Reinhold)

Gaius Julius Mygdonius, a Parthian by origin, born a free man, captured as a youth and sold into Roman territory. When I was made a citizen with the help of fate, I invested in a chest (made money) for the time I was fifty. Ever since youth I sought to reach old age; now receive me gladly, Stone; with you I shall be freed from care. (*Corpus of Latin Inscriptions* 11.137, Ravenna)

On May 24, 166 CE in the Roman province of Syria, on the coast of modern Lebanon, a low-ranking naval officer and a soldier made a contract. Gaius Fabullius Macer bought a slave from Quintus Julius Priscus. For 200 denarii, Macer acquired a healthy seven-year-old boy who came from Mesopotamia (across the Euphrates). For buyer and seller, this boy's name was not a fixed element of his identity. He was Abbas, which perhaps was his name at birth or some Latin or Greek version of it; he became Eutyches, which in Greek means "good luck," a common name for slaves; ultimately, however, the boy's name was a matter of who held him, sold him, or owned him. The contract raises many questions about the slave boy Abbas. Was the boy a captive seized in Rome's campaigns against Parthia, a powerful state outside the Roman empire in the northeastern area of modern Iran? How did he get from across the Euphrates to the coast of the Mediterranean? Had he been captured and sold to one of the slave dealers who followed the Roman armies, and then sold to Priscus who then sold him to Macer? Or had Priscus acquired him in a distribution of the plunder that fell to the victors? Where exactly was this boy born? Where did he grow up? What happened to his parents? Did he even understand what was happening to him beyond the separation from home and parents? The contract tells us only what was important for buyer and seller: his origin, his physical condition, his age, and his price – all required by the Edict of the Aediles, the Roman regulations governing the sale of slaves. The voice of the boy and his story are absent here: his history has been reduced to the facts relevant to sale.

By contrast, in the epitaph of Gaius Julius Mygdonius, buried in the city of Ravenna on the east coast of Italy probably in the first century CE, the ex-captive and ex-slave speaks. Mygdonius gives his readers a condensed biography whose events at least in his early years mirror those of Abbas. There was a battle, a raid, or transaction involving human goods. Among them was a freeborn youth separated from his family and his community in Parthia. Sold into Roman territory, he ended up in Italy, a world away from Parthia. We do not know what work he did but must assume he learned a new language and culture: his tombstone, written in Latin, suggests this. He received his freedom, he said, with fate's help. He made money, reached the goal of his youth, old age, and died. Again, the epitaph raises questions about the boy sold as a slave. Did he walk, chained perhaps, from somewhere across the Euphrates River to Roman territory where he was sold? Was Mygdonius his Parthian name or some Roman version of that name? Was he put on the raised platform used for slave sales with a label around his neck and his feet chalked, as was the practice with new captives? Was he poked, prodded, and made to strip? Was he ordered to open his mouth, so the buyer could smell his breath? Did he hear himself discussed in some language he did not understand? Who bought him? Who freed him? Although the epitaph speaks from the point of view of the ex-slave sold as a young boy, it, like the contract, records only the relevant "facts" – here facts relevant to the slave/ex-slave, not the buyer: his origin and free birth, his sale into the Roman empire, his manumission and Roman citizenship, his acquisition of a "chest" (of money or for burial) and his quest for old age. In effect, we have the beginning of his life as a slave and the end. Yet at that end, forty or so years after his capture and enslavement, he still remembered his origins as a free man and his birthplace and recorded them on his tombstone.

From different perspectives, the contract for the sale of Abbas and Mygdonius's tombstone tell us about the slave trade at Rome. More than indicating different points of view, the contract and tombstone delineate different positions in the sale of slaves – buyer, seller, and slave. The shape of a slave sale – what it was, what it meant, and how it was experienced, was configured by all three positions (see Johnson 1999). This chapter follows the sale of slaves from their initial enslavement, to their transport to market, to their preparation for sale, to the moment of sale in the market. At each stage, the focus is on the different activities, goals, and desires of soldiers and generals, slave traders and dealers, buyers, and finally slaves (I use the term "traders" to name those who collected slaves in provinces or from the armies, and "dealers" to talk about those who sold slaves in the marketplace).

In ancient Rome the sale of slaves, and the potential saleability of every slave, is significant for both the institution of slavery and the experience of slaves. Institutionally, a consideration of slave sales informs us about the supply of slaves: how war captives, victims of piracy, or home-born slaves were distributed to slave owners. The process of sale itself made human beings into human property. As noted in Chapter 2, the slave, like other forms of property, could be used in different ways: he or she was an item for sale, the repayment of or collateral for a loan, a gift, an item to be mortgaged, or an inheritance.

Ultimately, the slave sale stages what is central to the institution of chattel slavery: the slave is fungible – exchangeable, replaceable, substitutable; like cash, he or she can be turned to any use. The Roman poet Martial makes the point clearly, if cruelly:

> You sold a slave yesterday for 1,200 sesterces, Calliodorus, so that you could dine well one time. You have not dined well: the four-pound mullet that you bought was the set piece of your dinner. It's a pleasure to shout: "this is not a fish, a fish, you shameless man, it's a human being, Calliodorus, you eat up a human being." (10.31)

Martial scolds the imaginary Calliodorus not for selling a slave per se or for spending the money for something else, but for selling a slave and spending such a large chunk of change on a fish that he consumes at one dinner. In Martial's poem, the human being is turned into cash and the cash into a fish. The slave becomes a single fish eaten at dinner.

Slaves present a special problem in this discussion. Only a few dedications and epitaphs hint at the slave's experience in being sold. In his epitaph, Mygdonius, for example, outlines a kind of death as a freeborn Parthian and a rebirth as a Roman citizen; before that citizenship, however, would have been his rebirth as a slave in Roman territory. Other than these few inscriptions, our evidence for the slave's perspective is limited; there are no Roman slave narratives like those from the eighteenth- and the nineteenth-century Atlantic world of slavery, except the fictional autobiographical speech of Trimalchio, the wealthy ex-slave of Petronius's *Satyricon*. While we cannot reconstruct the meanings and experience of sale for Roman slaves from their own accounts, we can observe the conditions that shaped their experience – and imagine them as something more than commodities.

On the Battlefield: Generals and Soldiers

As noted in Chapter 2, individuals became slaves in a variety of ways: through capture by pirates, sale or abandonment by indigent parents, birth, and capture in war. Although the enslavement of Rome's defeated enemies was only one source of slaves, it was perhaps the most important source of slaves in the Republic and continued to supply slaves to Rome in the Principate. Moreover, the association between conquest and slavery shaped Roman perceptions of slaves and slavery. The jurist Florentinus (*Digest* 1.5.4.2) claims slaves were called *servi* because generals were accustomed to sell those captured in war (*captivos*), saving (*servare*) rather than killing them, and *mancipia* because they were seized from the enemy by force (*manu capiuntur*). Beside the captives, considered below, the important agents in this process of enslavement and initial sale are generals, soldiers, and traders.

After a successful battle or the sack of a city, the defeated were subdued, rounded up, and guarded. Depictions of the subjection of defeated enemies by Romans or their allies appear frequently in Roman art. The famous cameo called the Gemma Augustea, for example, celebrates Roman victories and the subjugation of the defeated (Figure 28). The upper register of the cameo depicts the emperor Augustus, his adopted son and the future emperor Tiberius, and Tiberius's adopted son Germanicus as the conquerors. On the lower level, Roman soldiers on the left, assisted by two bare-chested men, raise a trophy of arms. Two "barbarians" reflect different responses to capture – resentment and resignation. The man with long hair and a beard has his hands tied behind his back; he glares at his captors with anger. The woman rests her head in her hands, weary and resigned. Nearly a century later, on Trajan's Column, erected to celebrate the emperor's campaigns in Dacia (101–102, 105–106 CE), one of the scenes shows Dacian prisoners in a pen guarded by soldiers (Figure 29).

The commanding general determined the fate of these captives. The Romans considered captives part of the plunder, as Cicero does when in July of 54 BCE he writes to his friend Atticus about the possibilities of plunder from Caesar's invasion of Britain. He notes that there was not a bit of silver on the island and no hope of plunder (*praeda*) except slaves (*mancipia*) (4.16.7). The treatment of the defeated varied. When the Romans wanted to exact revenge, all were killed; in some

28. Gemma Augustea, Vienna, c. 15 CE. (Courtesy of the Kunsthistorische Museum, Vienna)

instances, the enemy leaders or those who had opposed the Romans were killed, and the rest sold into slavery; in others, the defeated, especially those who had aided the Romans, were freed or ransomed to relatives or friends who could pay. However, death or sale seems to have been the most common fate of the conquered. At Corinth in 146 BCE, for example, as at many other places in the history of Rome's wars in the Mediterranean, the Roman general ordered the adult men killed and the women and children sold into slavery (Pausanias 7.16.8).

Not infrequently, the general awarded captives to his soldiers as plunder, often as an acknowledgment of their courage and martial virtue – what the Romans called *virtus*. After the defeat of Gallic chief Vercingetorix at Alesia in 52 BCE, for instance, Julius Caesar distributed as plunder one captive to each soldier in his army (Caesar, *Gallic*

29. Penned Dacians on Trajan's Column, Rome, 113 CE. (su concessione del Minstero per i Beni e le Attività Culturali – Soprintendenza Speciale per i Beni Archeologici di Roma)

War 7.89). By the second half of the first century CE, a chain with manacles may have been part of the standard equipment of the Roman soldier, used to bind captives to their captors. Several reliefs, presumably celebrating their success, show Roman soldiers holding the conquered by a chain (Figures 30a and b).

Usually, however, soldiers received some of the moveable objects of the plunder, and the general handed over the captives to his quaestor (a magistrate charged with financial matters) to be sold at auction to traders who followed the armies. Cicero's behavior after his small victory at Pindemissum during his governorship of Cilicia was typical. He gave his soldiers all the plunder except the captives, whom he sold on December 19, 51 BCE: "as I write, there is about 120,000 sesterces on the platform" (*Letters to Atticus* 5.20.5).

30. (a) Soldier with prisoner in chains on the Arch of Septimius Severus, Rome, 203 CE. (Scala/Art Resource, New York) (b) Soldier with prisoners in chains on a tomb relief, Nickenich, c. 60 CE. (Photo Rheinisches Landesmuesum, Bonn)

The Romans referred to the auction of the conquered as sale *sub hasta* (under the spear) or *sub corona* (under the wreath/garland). Explaining a legal procedure for claiming property, the jurist Gaius in the second century CE explains that the plaintiff touched the "thing" claimed (his example is a slave) with a rod that represented a spear, the symbol of lawful ownership (*iustum dominium*) because the Romans thought that things that they had seized from the enemy were lawfully theirs (*Institutes* 4.16). The person enslaved in war was not simply something captured from the enemy; he or she had been the enemy.

Thus, in court this ritual replaced the act of violent seizure and sale on the battlefield. The legal practice made every slave, captured in war or home born, a conquered foreigner whose powerlessness had been manifest in capture. Aulus Gellius, a writer and collector of stories in the second century CE, reports that slaves (*mancipia*) seized by right of war were sold wearing *coronae* and so said to be sold *sub corona;* the garland meant that those sold were captives (*Attic Nights* 6.4.2–3). Spear or garland, each signaled the defeat of the captive and his or her degradation to a person for sale to the highest bidder. It is not simply that the spear or the garland was a sign of defeat; the practice of sale under the sign marked a step in the commodification of the human sold – a step toward fungibility. Cicero did not even count the captives that he put up for sale; for him, they were 120,000 sesterces.

Indeed, captives enslaved in war had varied meanings for soldiers, generals, the state, and slave traders. For the individual soldier who received a captive as part of the plunder, the captive was a material sign of his own *virtus*. When he kept the captive as a slave, he gained labor that he might use on his farm or in his household. When he sold the captive to the traders who followed the armies, the captive became cash.

For generals, captives were a means to reward soldiers for their valor and a material manifestation of their own *virtus* and glory. Successful generals usually reserved some of the conquered, especially the most important prisoners, and sent them to Rome to march in their triumphs, the processions that celebrated their own *virtus* and Rome's military might. In epitaphs or honorary inscriptions that recount the deeds of Rome's great men, generals proudly noted the taking of captives. The historian Livy describes a tablet in the shape of Sardinia with painted depictions of battles from the Sardinian campaigns of Tiberius Sempronius Gracchus: on it Gracchus boasts that "Under the command and auspices of Tiberius Sempronius Gracchus, the legion and army of the Roman people subjugated Sardinia. In that province more than 80,000 of the enemy were killed or captured" (*History of Rome* 41.28.9–10). For generals, captives, too, were money: as noted above, the people sold by Cicero in 51 BCE became 120,000 sesterces. Cicero turned the funds over to the state. Other commanders used the money gained from the auction of captives for material manifestations of their glory: what was not given to the state was spent on games, distributions, and buildings.

Captives had similar meanings for the Roman state and its citizens. In Roman histories of Rome's wars, the pattern of recording the number of people captured and sold measures Rome's military success. The citizens of Rome celebrated the glory of their state and vicariously participated in the power of Roman armies by watching the chained captives pass before them in the spectacle of the triumph (see Figure 24). Captives became cash for the state's expenses that included waging other wars. Thus, enslaved captives became gifts of the general to his troops, signs of their valor and the success of Rome, funds for the state, and even monuments in the city of Rome.

On the Battlefield: Slaves

Capture in battle for the defeated was surrounded by loss, violence, and death. What for the Roman soldier and general was *virtus,* for the captive soldier was his own loss of valor, and, in the case of some of the peoples conquered by the Romans, a loss of honor. For all, capture in war was an event preceded by the violence of battle or the deprivations of a siege. It meant the death or injury of family and friends. It meant destroyed homes, cities, and farms. The sack of a city by the Romans could be a terrifying experience. The Greek historian of Rome, Polybius, who admired the Romans, describes what he believes to be the common pattern of a Roman sack. He remarks that "one can often see in cities taken by the Romans not only the bodies of human beings, but dogs cut in half and the severed limbs of other animals" (10.15.5). For women and boys, rape was a common fate.

One of the scenes on Trajan's Column, which depicts the emperor's campaigns in Dacia, gives a glimpse of the fate of conquered men,

31. Attack on a Dacian village on Trajan's Column, Rome, 113 CE. (su concessione del Minstero per i Beni e le Attività Culturali – Soprintendenza Speciale per i Beni Archeologici di Roma)

women, children, and animals (Figure 31). On the lower left, Roman auxiliaries kill the men of a Dacian village; one man with a child flees the scene. Above cavalry set fire to the houses of the village. Next to them, Trajan, apparently addressing a woman with a child, points to a ship, while below him soldiers drive Dacian women with children toward the Danube River where ships will take them away from their homes. Slaughtered animals are piled up beneath an overhanging rock.

After the violence of war came physical imprisonment: the defeated were penned up like the Dacians herded into an enclosure in a scene on Trajan's Column (Figure 29) or chained like the defeated men in Figure 30. Although we cannot know the thoughts of prisoners like those Dacians in Figure 29, it is a useful exercise to shift the point of view of the relief that depicts the captives from outside the pen to the point of view of the prisoners crowded together and looking out toward their captors. The effect of chaining could be humiliating to the point of stupefaction. In 191 BCE, reports the historian Polybius, the Roman consul, frustrated in his dealings with the Aetolians, ordered his men to bring out chains and to bind the neck of every man in the Aetolian embassy with an iron collar, even though these men were not only free Greeks but upper-class citizens of Aetolia. The Aetolians, says Polybius, were awed, speechless as if they were paralyzed in both body and mind (*Histories* 20.10.7–9).

If the Romans understood the sale of prisoners *sub corona* or *sub hasta* as dishonoring, it may well be that the defeated, even if they did not share the Roman perspective, experienced the practice as denigrating and/or shameful. This first transaction as well as the reward of prisoners to soldiers will have resulted in further separation from family for those sold to different traders or given to different soldiers. For all, it meant a further separation from community. The battlefield and its aftermath, too, marked the beginning of the end of everything war prisoners knew about social rules and order, identity, manners, and sexuality; from this point forward, as slaves, they were thrust into a new set of rules. These first losses of family, community, and culture meant the death of a social life among family, friends, neighbors, and citizens or tribal members – hence, the first stage of what historians of slavery call "social death" (see Chapter 2).

On the Road: Slave Traders

Traders not only followed the armies, buying captives at auction on the battlefield; they also followed trade routes established long before Roman conquests, acquiring slaves from a variety of sources – pirates, local markets, and the long-distance trade from outside the empire. Slaves acquired in one place might be resold to other traders who sold them in local markets or transported them to one of the larger markets in the Mediterranean world: Byzantium, Delos, Ephesus, Puteoli, and, of course, the city of Rome. The legal sources suggest that slave traders worked in partnerships, with one or more partners in the provinces collecting slaves, and the other selling them in the marketplace. Cicero, for example, mentions a Lucius Publicius who arrived in Etruria (modern Tuscany) with slaves from Gaul for sale in 83 BCE – well before Caesar's campaigns there in the 50s BCE and probably the result of wars between various tribes in Gaul (*In Defense of Quinctius* 24). In his encyclopedia of the natural world, Pliny the Elder recounts the story of a slave dealer of the late first century BCE, Toranius Flaccus, who sold Marc Antony two handsome boys for 200,000 sesterces, claiming they were twins, although one boy came from Asia Minor and the other from north of the Alps. Flaccus or his agents had gathered these slaves from both sides of the empire.

The transport of slaves to the market where they were finally sold to buyers would often have been long and arduous, whether they walked overland or were shipped by sea. The trader who acquired the young Parthian boy, Mygdonius, for example, may have taken him by land to one of the markets on the coast like the city of Ephesus; whoever bought him there, or perhaps the trader, took him overland or shipped him to Italy across the Mediterranean. Chaining slaves by neck shackles and linking chains in transport was common. In Plautus's comedy *The Captives,* a man who has purchased two war captives from the quaestor arrives at home and orders his steward to take off the heavy chains that couple them together and put on lighter ones, reminding him to keep a close watch: "A free captive is like a wild bird; if he is once given the chance to flee, that is enough; you can never take hold of him afterwards" (116–18). Plautus's lines may seem like merely an adage, but two centuries later the Roman jurist Labeo indicates that they were no simple fiction: he mentions a partner in a slave-dealing business who was wounded trying to prevent the slaves kept for sale from breaking out and escaping (*Digest* 17.2.60.1).

The tombstone of Aulus Capreilius Timotheus, identified in Greek as a slave dealer (*somatemporos*), found at Amphipolis, depicts a line of eight male slaves chained at the neck, followed by two unchained women and two children and led by a man in a hooded cloak, the slave dealer himself or a guard (Figure 32). Although these captives and

32. Relief of chained slaves on the Tomb of Aulus Capreilius Timotheus,
Amphipolis. (From H. Duchêne, "Sur la stèle d'Aulus Caprilius Timotheos
Sômatemporos," *Bulletin de Correspondance Hellénique* 110 [1986], p. 517, fig. 3)

their relations to each other are not named, the relief presents a line
of people organized by gender and age for the purpose of supervision
and control. The men are chained because they were presumed to offer
the most resistance; the women are not perhaps because they seemed
to pose no danger or because they were attached by familial bonds to
the men or the children; and the latter would have had nowhere to go
without the adults (who may well have been their parents).

The evidence for slave traders themselves as well as the dealers who
sold slaves in the market is rather sparse. Only a few are named in the
literary sources; dedications and epitaphs, like Capreilius's, give us several dozen more names. Some traders are difficult to identify because
they dealt in several commodities, including slaves. In Petronius's novel,
the wealthy freedman Trimalchio recounts that after losing five ships at

sea, he built more, loaded them up with wine, lard, beans, ointment, and slaves, and made a fortune (76.6). Petronius depicts Trimalchio as crass, and the freedman's admission marks his vulgarity, for slave dealers were renowned for their greed and dishonesty. This reputation, especially for men with aspirations of respectability, may explain their reticence in identifying themselves as slave traders. This stain, however, did not affect men like Aulus Capreilius Timotheus, who not only claimed the trade but also depicted it on his tombstone. Capreilius was a freed slave, as were several other known slave dealers; legal status limited their claims to respectability. Other dealers, however, were freeborn and Roman citizens, although none of them belonged to the social elite, as far as we can tell.

Traders like Capreilius who acquired slaves on the battlefield or in the provinces and transported them to market acquired goods for sale – commodities – and, as such, slaves were fungible. Although the jurists make a technical distinction that separates slaves from other commodities or goods (*merces*), that distinction is not always clear, and it certainly did not erase the slave's fungibility (*Digest* 50.16.207). As the jurist Gaius observes, Roman law equates slaves and animals: "it … appears that the statute treats equally our slaves and our four-footed cattle which are kept in herds, such as sheep, goats, horses, mules, and asses" (*Digest* 9.2.2.2). In effect, as far as the legal rules were concerned, one animal could be substituted for another in the list, including human animals. The historian Diodorus Siculus makes clear the fungibility of the people collected by traders for sale, when he says that merchants, playing on the Gauls' love of wine, traded an amphora of wine for a slave, thus exchanging the drink for the cupbearer (5.26.3). The treatment of slaves en route to market – penning, chaining, marching them overland, or shipping them by sea – certainly handled them as merchandise. Petronius's Trimalchio bespeaks the common assumption: wine, lard, beans, ointment, and slaves were all equally merchandise. We might also see that traders' practices not only dealt with human beings as merchandise; in effect, they made them merchandise. In other words, the slave's fungibility is evident in and created by the practices of traders.

On the Road: Slaves

Chains, long enforced marches, and the general hardship of travel took their toll on captives. Transport by ship was dangerous, and the legal sources mention slaves lost by drowning and illness. The various remedies and treatments used by slave dealers in preparing slaves for market suggest the need to repair damage incurred in overland travel – weight loss, exhaustion, and injury. Iron collars caused pain or constant discomfort, and walking along chained to others, like the chained slaves in the relief on Capreilius's tomb, made travel awkward, to say the least. The sculptor depicts men of different heights, walking at different paces; some are crowded together, and others strung out a bit more. Either the chained slaves struggled along, or perhaps, although forced by circumstances, they learned to cooperate. We cannot know whether they gained some sense of sharing or community from their common fate, or whether they felt only irritation or anger directed at the short man or the slow man on the chain.

The historian of Roman slavery Keith Bradley has suggested just how disorienting such journeys would have been in a world where few educated Romans, much less ordinary people from the areas of Roman conquests, had even the most basic geographical knowledge. Talking about captives taken in Caesar's campaigns in Britain in 55 and 54 BCE, he observes:

> Their forced journey, by sea to the Continent and then overland to Italy, would have taken them across a vast region of which they could previously have had hardly any detailed knowledge or awareness – they were, quite literally, travelling into the unknown, in a timeless and directionless way, with no prospect of ever returning – and along the route they would probably have been sold several times from dealer to dealer. (Bradley 1994: 46)

In light of this experience, it is not surprising that few slaves and ex-slaves, like Mygdonius, the freed slave from Parthia discussed above, named their places of origin on their tombstones. Some scholars argue that slaves and ex-slaves wanted to depict themselves as fitting into the new world in which they found themselves. However, if Bradley is correct about the experience of travel to the market, home was in a fundamental way lost in the "timeless and directionless" trip through an unknown landscape.

If traders' treatment of captives on their way to market made them commodities, each step toward fungibility also moved them along the road toward "natal alienation." Historians use the term to indicate the slave's loss of blood ties to parents, grandparents, and children and the loss of native status – an attachment to particular groups and a particular place. In other words, transport to market took slaves further along the road of social death. The route taken by Abbas or Mygdonius led them further and further from home, as it did captives taken in Caesar's invasion of Britain. Each mile traveled and each sale along the route separated captives from family and their fellows. The trip itself severed captives from the original markers of their identity – family, community, language, land, or landscape.

Along the road, or later in the market, or even later in an owner's house, or perhaps several times over, the slave lost another significant marker of identity – his or her name. The seven-year-old boy, sold in 166 CE in Roman Syria, was Abbas, Eutyches, or "whatever other name he is called." The writer Varro comments on this shift of names:

So, when three men have bought a slave each at Ephesus, sometimes one derives the name (of the slave) from Artemidorus, the man who sold the slaves, and thus calls his slave Artemas; another names his slave Ion from the region Ionia, because he bought him there; the other names his slave Ephesius, because he bought him at Ephesus. So each man chooses a name from one source or another, however it seems right to him. (*The Latin Language* 8.21, trans. R. G. Kent)

Here slaveholders chose names from the slave's history of sale – from the seller or from the region or city in which the slave was purchased. In early Rome, slave owners (re)named a male slave by combining the Latin word for boy (*puer*), regardless of the slave's age, and the genitive of his owner's name (that is, his owner's name in the case indicating possession): Marcipor, for example, was *Marci puer* (Marcus's boy). Later, in addition to the practices described by Varro, Romans used a limited list of Latin or more commonly Greek names for slaves, whatever the slave's origin. Names like Eros (love), Fides (trust, good faith), Hilarus (cheerful), or Felix (lucky) imprinted the owner's hopes or fantasies on the slave. For buyer and seller, as Varro observes, this was a matter of "however it seems right to him." For the captive, this (re) naming meant the loss of the name he or she was given at birth, and sale or transfer to a new owner might repeat the loss. The sociologist Orlando Patterson sees the change of the slave's name as part of the ritual of enslavement: "the changing of a name is almost universally a symbolic act of stripping a person of his former identity. ...The slave's former name died with his former self" (1982: 54–58, esp. 55).

At the end of the road were the market and a master. Sold to a buyer, the captive became the slave of an individual and entered into the slave's only social relationship acknowledged by Roman society. The practices of the marketplace firmly confronted the captive with his or her status as a fungible object – something for sale to be put to a use determined by the seller and the buyer.

In the Marketplace: Sellers

The slave market was an institution with all the practices and rules of other marketplaces. Dedications to the *genius venalicii,* the spirit of the slave market, by individuals who probably sold in the market suggest normal religious practice. Individuals like the emperor or the head of a household, self-help societies (*collegia*), groups of individuals, especially those with the same occupation, places, and institutions where Romans carried on particular activities all had their own *genius* (spirit). Like the society of wine merchants and the wine market at Ostia, the slave market in Rome had its *genius*. The sale of slaves, too, had rules laid out in the Edict of the Aediles, mentioned in the contract for the sale of Abbas discussed above. Revised and added to over time, the Edict dictated the information that the seller had to give the buyer, protected the buyer from the seller's fraud, and set the condition for the return of a slave or the recovery of part of the buyer's cost. Basically, the seller had to tell the buyer of the slave's defects or diseases; he had to inform the buyer if the slave was a runaway or a loiterer; he had to report any capital offenses done by the slave, if the slave was subject to damages incurred by his actions, if he had been condemned to fight wild animals in the arena as punishment, and if he had made any attempts on his own life (*Digest* 21.1.1.1). In addition, as pointed out in Chapter 2, the seller had to state the origin of every slave that he sold (21.1.31.21).

The most important market in Rome was behind the Temple of Castor in the Roman Forum (Map 4). Here slave merchants dealt in varieties of slaves; Seneca claims their shops were crammed with a crowd of the lowliest slaves (*On Firmness* 13.4). By the second half of the first century CE, buyers went to the Saepta Julia in the Campus Martius for fancier slaves, especially boys sold for sexual purposes. Martial describes a man named Mamurra strolling through the Saepta, "where golden Rome ravages its wealth" – that is, where buyers consumed the luxury goods that empire brought to the city (Map 4). There, amid fancy tables, precious statues, bronze ware, crystal vases, elegant dinnerware, emeralds, pearls, and sardonyxes, the wealthy could find "soft boys" – some on display, but the best hidden away in the back of the shops (9.59).

Slave dealers prepared slaves for sale. In his encyclopedia of the natural world, Pliny the Elder notes the uses of various plant and animal products for improving the servile body for sale. For emaciated slaves, slave dealers applied resin from the terebinth tree that supposedly relaxed the skin, so that the slave could be plumped out by food (*Natural History*

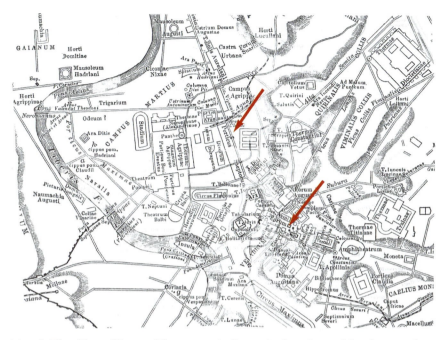

Map 4. The City of Rome. The arrows indicate the locations of the slave market behind the Temple of Castor in the Roman Forum and the Saepta where buyers could purchase luxury goods, including fancy slaves. (From S. B. Platner, *The Topography and Monuments of Ancient Rome* [Boston: Allyn and Bacon, 1911], frontispiece)

24.35). To make boys look younger, the slave dealer used depilatories prepared with the blood, gall, and liver of tuna (32.135). The root of hyacinth mixed with sweet wine slowed the signs of puberty and inhibited boys' sexual development (21.170). The great teacher of oratory Quintilian cites Plato, who, the Roman orator says, sees the skill of slave dealers as faking the results of exercise because they simulate color by dye and real strength by useless fattening (*Oratorical Training* 2.15.25). What could not be fixed could be hidden: dealers covered or decked out in finery wounds, scars, or other bodily flaws. In what the Romans regarded as an extreme manipulation of the male body, some boys were castrated, and castration itself was called the slave dealer's art

33. Slave sale on a tombstone, Capua, late first century CE. (G. Fittschen Neg. D-DAI-Rom 1983VW1305)

(*ars mangonis;* Martial 9.6). Domitian banned the castration of slaves on Roman soil, but the practice continued, and two later emperors continued to find it necessary to legislate against it.

The slave stood on a platform called a *catasta* (Figure 33). A label with the relevant information about the slave hung around his or her neck. New captives had their feet chalked to mark their condition. Some were made to leap around to demonstrate their health or agility. Sometimes the buyer would order the slave stripped, and he or the dealer would poke or prod the slave to check for defects or flaws (see below). The dealer also might demonstrate the quality of the slave. In one of Martial's poems, an auctioneer, trying to sell a girl of lowly reputation, grabs her and kisses her four times to show that her mouth is clean – that is, that she has not been performing oral sex (6.66).

The slave dealer made his sales pitch in a loud voice. In one of his poems, Horace compares a typical slave dealer's sales pitch to his own unfilled promise to write letters to the addressee of the poem. Like Horace's promise, the sales pitch technically avoids misrepresentation, however deceptive it may be:

> Suppose anyone really wanted to sell you a boy born at Tibur or Gabii and made this pitch to you. "He is fair and handsome from the top of his head to the bottom of his feet. And he will be yours for 8,000 sesterces. This home-born slave is prepared to serve at his master's nod. He knows a little Greek; he is suitable for whatever task you want. With this wet clay, you can make whatever you please. He even can sing something untrained but sweet, when you are drinking. Many promises lessen the buyer's trust, when someone who wants to get rid of his goods praises a slave on sale more lavishly than is right. Nothing forces me to sell. I am not rich but I am not in debt. None of the slave dealers would do this for you, and I would not do this for everybody. Once he shirked his work, and, you know how it is, he hid under the stairs, afraid of the whip hanging on the wall." (*Letters* 2.2.1–19)

Here is the language of one human being (at least a Roman one) who tries to sell a human being to another human being. We get a laundry list of qualities – for a personal servant, it should be noted, not a field hand: the dealer showcases appearance, origin, potential, if not exactly skill, and he admits a flaw. The dealer crafts an image of the boy attractive to the buyer, imagining for him a pretty, malleable human commodity, ready and able to serve. The metaphor of wet clay directly expresses the slave's fungibility and appeals to the power of the master to mold the slave to his own use. Shaping the boy to suit the buyer, the seller slips around the facts of the boy's life. He slyly claims that the boy, born in Italy, knows a little Greek and has a nice, if untrained, voice; technically, a little Greek might mean a word or two and his musicality precludes any real skill. Sly, too, is his admission not of flight but of a single episode of hiding out, such as might happen to any boy. Legally, the seller had to tell the buyer if a slave was a runaway or a loiterer; Horace's seller finesses the requirement by owning up to one instance. The admission only serves to sell the slave, for any slave afraid of the lash is one who, as the dealer advertises, reacts to the nod of his master. The dealer ends by flattering the buyer: no other dealer would make him this offer, and he certainly would not make such an offer to anyone else.

In literature and law, slave dealers were renown for their deception and greed. To get rid of his merchandise, the dealer applied cosmetics, resorted to medical tricks, covered flaws, disguised the "real" slave. In his sales pitch and claims about the slave, he lied or, like Horace's imaginary dealer, skirted the line of truth to avoid legal action. Also, in another form of lying, he pushed his goods by flattering the buyer, and his flattery was often depicted as servile like the goods he sells. Whether because of their greed, their trickiness, or their trafficking in people, dealers were also seen as dirty. Martial's auctioneer who kisses a slave girl to show that she is clean only dirties her: the one bid that had been made for her is immediately withdrawn after the dealer's demonstration.

In the end, dealers sold people for a price: Abbas for 200 denarii; the two boys that Toranius Flaccus sold to Antony as twins for 200,000 sesterces; the boy from Tibur or Gabii in Horace's poem for 8,000 sesterces; the girl kissed by Martial's auctioneer for 600 sesterces. Price reduced human difference to cash amounts: each person sold became his or her price and a fungible, malleable commodity. By the scale of sesterces and denarii, dealers could compare the Mesopotamian seven-year-old Abbas to, if not interchange him with, Horace's Italian boy or Flaccus's so-called twins from Asia Minor and the Alps.

In the Marketplace: Buyers

Buyers looked at the slaves on sale with a piercing gaze – indeed, an invasive gaze. Martial's Mamurra who peruses the Saepta Julia, shopping for all the luxurious goodies that imperial Rome offers its wealthy inhabitants, eats up the boys on sale with his eyes (9.59). As noted above, sellers inspected slaves physically, poking, prodding, and demanding that slaves be stripped of their clothing. "When you buy a horse," explains Seneca, "you order its blanket to be removed; you pull off the garments from slaves that are up for sale, so that no bodily flaws may escape your notice." Since slave dealers hid defects under fancy trappings, a covered-up leg or arm aroused suspicion, and "you order that it be stripped and the body itself be shown to you" (*Letters* 80.9).

The Romans have not left any letters in which prospective buyers discuss what they hoped to find in the slave market, but Roman literature is full of passages that describe the use of slaves and the kind of slaves needed for one task or another, and in this way it allows us to glimpse the assumptions that buyers brought to the slave market. The Edict of the Aediles that regulated the sale of slaves, too, is a useful guide to the concerns of buyers. Commenting on the Edict, the lawyers spent a lot of time sorting out the difference between diseases and defects in slaves put up for sale. Their comments mirror the concerns of buyers and help us to think about the desires, standards, and expectations of buyers. Putting together these sources, we can divide these concerns into the slave's history, physical condition and speech, mental state and behavior, and occupation.

As noted earlier, the slave's place of origin interested buyers as an index of character and behavior. Imagine, for example, Marcus Terentius Varro at the slave market near the Temple of Castor in Rome. His manual on agriculture, written in the late first century BCE, includes advice on the kinds of slaves fit for different tasks on the farm and suggest the standards that he, or a reader following his advice, applied in the slave market. He would pay close attention to origin in his selecting slaves. First, he would calculate the origins of the slaves that he already owned, so as not to buy too many from one place, because, according to Varro, too many slaves from the same place caused "domestic quarrels" (*On Agriculture* 1.17.5). Second, origin was a yardstick of potential. If the buyer was in the market for herdsmen, he should choose Gauls and avoid Bastulans or Turdulans (peoples from southern Spain): "It is not every people that is fitted to herding; thus neither a Bastulan nor a Turdulan is suited, while Gauls are admirably adapted especially for draft animals" (2.10.4). If he wanted female slaves as mates for his herdsmen, he would do well to consider slaves from Illyricum, as these women were "strong and not ill-looking [and] as fit for work as men" (2.10.7).

Cicero, Varro's contemporary, indicates the importance of origin for other kinds of slaves. Writing to his friend Atticus in November 55 BCE, he jokes about the potential captives from Caesar's invasion of Britain: "I think that you will not expect any of *them* to be learned in literature or music" (*Letters to Atticus* 4.16.7). Cicero assumes a common perception of Britons: any buyer who goes to market to buy a personal servant, secretary, or musician would eliminate any Briton on the *catasta*. Origin even entered the considerations of men in the market for a sexual favorite: fantasizing about his ideal, the poet Martial chooses a boy from Egypt because of its reputation for sexual wantonness (4.42).

A man's or woman's experience of slavery, too, entered buyers' considerations, for the slave's past affected his or her future use and subordination. The Edict of the Aediles set out the common assumption: "it is assumed that the more recently he has been enslaved, the slave will be more malleable, more trainable to his function, more responsive to directions, and more adaptable to any service; on the other hand it is difficult to retrain an experienced slave or one of long standing and to mold his habits." Here the buyer had to be especially concerned with the "tricks of dealers." Since the newly enslaved brought a higher price and "since slave dealers know that their customers will readily seek to purchase new slaves, they interpose those of long standing and sell them as new" (*Digest* 21.1.37).

To judge from the extensive list of physical traits and ailments covered in the Edict of the Aediles, the physical condition and health of slaves preoccupied buyers. Nearly every part of the body merited consideration, and, we must assume, an examination that probed every part of the slave body or subjected it to public view. Buyers looked to see if the slave was hunchbacked or deformed, prone to itch, covered with scales, a bed-wetter, left-handed, or suffering from impetigo or warts, or, even more seriously, fever, gout, or epilepsy. They checked for varicose veins, cuts on arms and legs, scars, and missing, fused, or extra toes and fingers. The head seems to have received scrupulous attention: different sized jaws, protruding eyes, bad breath, missing tongues or teeth, and swollen tonsils. Part of the physical examination was gendered. Was a male slave missing a testicle or was he a eunuch? Was a female slave barren or too tight for sexual intercourse, did she give birth to stillborn babies, did she menstruate twice a month or not at all? Buyers were concerned with slaves' ability to use their senses: was the slave deaf, dumb, blind, shortsighted, or one-eyed? Buyers also wanted to know if the slave spoke with difficulty or gutturally, raved, rambled, stammered, or lisped.

Buyers who came to the market with specific jobs in mind saw slaves' physical condition and age in terms of their intended use. To return to Varro, if the buyer was looking for herdsmen, he wanted men whose limbs were supple and who were sturdy, swift, and nimble; boys were fine for smaller animals, but for cattle the slaveholder needed older men (*On Agriculture* 2.10.1–3). About a century later, Columella in his own agricultural manual recommends that a plowman have a big voice and an imposing bearing. Those who work in the vineyards need brawn and wide shoulders. Common laborers can be any height, as long as they can endure hard work (1.9). As Martial makes clear, slaves intended for work on the farm can be short-haired, unkempt, unsophisticated, and small, but not so slaves chosen to wait on a wealthy man's table (10.98.8–10): for such tasks the buyer looked for physical beauty. So, too, did men purchasing slave boys for sexual use. In Martial's poem on his ideal boy, he makes a shopping list of features that the purchaser of a sexual favorite might seek: fair skin, shiny eyes, low brow, narrow nose, long, unbraided hair, and red lips (4.42).

Last, buyers were interested in slaves' mental condition and behavior. No one wanted to buy a slave who had tried to commit suicide or constantly ran away, and buyers needed to know if the slave was likely to wander or loiter. Equally problematic were slaves who were thieves, gamblers, religious fanatics, corpse robbers, gluttons, wine drinkers, impostors, or liars. Buyers apparently asked about fits of depression or madness. The Edict lays out sets of qualities that distinguished the bad slave from the good slave. The bad slave was fickle, wanton, slothful, sluggish, idle, tardy, timorous, greedy, quick-tempered, frivolous, superstitious, and obstinate. The good slave was loyal, hardworking, diligent, and vigilant (*Digest* 21.1).

Slaves' mental qualities and behavior, like their physical condition, weighed on buyers' minds as they assessed slaves for particular uses. Along with their strength, stature, and age, Varro considered the character of the slaves working on his farms: they should be neither timid nor haughty; the overseer had to be dependable as well as older than those he supervised (and he needed to know how to read and write; *On Agriculture* 1.17.3–4). Columella, too, judged minds as well as bodies in selecting slaves for particular tasks: shepherds had to be diligent and thrifty; the big-voiced, tall plowman had to be terrifying (to the oxen) but not cruel (1.9).

The law specified the seller's responsibilities when he sold a slave with a specific occupation. If he claimed the slave was the best cook, the slave had to meet that standard, but if the dealer claimed only that the slave could cook, a mediocre cook would do (*Digest* 21.1.18.1); similarly, if he stated that the slave was a craftsman, he needed to be only an adequate craftsman. Although the ideal slave was honest, faithful, and hardworking, these qualities counted where they were useful, as Cicero makes clear in one of his speeches: "when we are buying slaves, we are annoyed if we have bought a man as a smith or a plasterer, and find that, however honest a man he is, he knows nothing of those trades that we sought in buying him; if we have bought a man whom we make a manager or put in charge of our livestock, then we care about nothing in him except frugality, industry, and vigilance" (*In Defense of Plancius* 62). In other circumstances, certain qualities added up to a particular occupation in the buyer's mind, or as in Horace's imaginary sales pitch, the slave's qualities simply made him "wet clay" – ready to be shaped in whatever way pleased his new owner.

Buyers faced sellers across the body and person of the slave. From the point of view of buyers, the relationship was infused with distrust. The accusation that dealers were greedy, tricky, and even dirty stigmatized slave dealers and absolved slave buyers. The gaze and examination of the buyer were invasive and intrusive: when emperors ogled or groped proper Roman matrons and girls, they abused their power and dishonored such women. However, the practice applied to slaves was acceptable – indeed, a matter of fact. The excuse for the buyer's visual and physical investigation was that slave dealers cheated, and the buyer had to protect himself from the tricks of the dealer to make sure that he got what was advertised. In this way, buyers were distanced from the manipulation of bodies and their display on the *catasta,* and they were able to see their own activities as the rational acquisition of a cheap labor force as Cato the Elder did when he bought war captives at a cheap price (Plutarch, *Life of Cato* 4.4, 21.1) or as the discerning judgment of a connoisseur as Pliny did (see below).

Yet the activities of slave dealers were intertwined with buyers in ways that made the slave fungible for each of them, albeit in different ways. No less for buyer than seller, the slave *was* his or her price, and thus comparable to any other slave, despite differences of age, sex, origin, appearance, or, for that matter, species. When Seneca compares pulling a blanket off a horse for sale to undressing a slave in the market, he makes clear that for the buyer the slave was a commodity. We might say that this sort of inspection made the person like a horse – an object for sale.

Buyers also saw slaves in terms of the varied needs, desires, and objectives that they or their agents brought to the market. Some men bought slaves for investment, others for labor, and still others for sexual pleasure. Horace's slave dealer appeals to what he supposes is the buyer's fantasy of a house servant; Martial's poem on the ideal boy spells out the fantasy of a sexual companion. As Cicero makes clear, the buyer who wanted a craftsman had one image in his mind; the man who wanted an overseer had another. These notions had everything to do with the buyer and nothing to do with the real slave on offer. Whatever the real slave before him on the *catasta,* the buyer read the slave with eyes and hands for the plowman, herdsman, overseer, personal servant, craftsman, or sexual favorite he had come to purchase. To the extent that the slave seemed to fit the buyer's purposes, he or she became the imagined plowman, herdsman, overseer, personal servant, craftsman, or sexual favorite.

The buyer not only purchased his own idea of a workman, servant, or companion; in the slave or in the act of purchase he also got a certain image of himself. According to Pliny the Elder, when Antony found out the twins he had bought for 200,000 sesterces were not twins at all but boys born in two different places, he was furious. The slave dealer Toranius Flaccus explained that twins who looked alike were not remarkable, but two boys with the same appearance from different places were beyond evaluation. The explanation won over the furious Antony who now considered nothing among his possessions to be more suited to his rank. Pliny calls Flaccus "cunning," but the cunning lies in crafting a story about the boys that compliments the buyer – indeed, makes him a certain kind of man.

A letter from Pliny the Younger to a friend from his hometown of Comum in northern Italy indicates a different side of fungibility:

> I have the highest possible opinion of your judgment and critical eye, not because your taste is so *very* good (don't flatter yourself) but because it is as good as mine. Joking apart, I think the slaves you advised me to buy look all right, but it remains to be seen if they are honest and here one can't go by a

slave's looks, but rather by what one hears of him. (1.21, trans.
B. Radice, *LCL*)

Pliny compliments his friend and himself on their mutual good judgment. As with Antony in Pliny the Elder's tale, the purchase of slaves is
the grounds for a man's sense of self. Pliny fashions himself as a man of
taste and discernment – and his friend, too, although only because his
taste is the same as his own. Pliny, however, goes beyond his friend's
standards, reminding him that although the slaves look fine, their hon-
esty remains to be tested, and that can be judged with one's ears, not
one's eyes. Beyond the image of self constructed in the purchase of
slaves, Pliny expresses and even shapes his friendship, with its competi-
tive edge, through the bodies of the slaves that he has purchased.

In the Marketplace: Slaves

From our point of view, slaves' sale in the market is the most con-
spicuous instance of fungibility: their bodies, lives, origins, and skills,
real and imagined, fully became objects of exchange. Penned up and
readied for sale, slaves in Rome were fattened, painted, slathered with
this or that concoction, and dressed up; the dealer or his agent covered up wounds and scars and chalked the feet of new captives. The
slave climbed onto the *catasta* to be prodded, poked, unclothed – the
object of the piercing gaze of onlookers and buyers. As noted above,
the Romans themselves regarded these actions as humiliating. Roman
authors can imagine the shame of the castrated boy. The chalked feet of
the new captive were regarded as a stain that carried over into freedom
long after any trace of chalk remained. How slaves themselves experienced what the Romans saw as shameful is unrecorded. The culture
from which a slave came will have shaped that experience. However,
we can ask whether some of the Romans' own perspective infused
the scene of sale. A home-born slave or a slave who had lived within
Roman society would certainly have known the denigration Roman

culture attached to the practices of the slave market, and the new captive eventually learnt it.

The slave dealer's pitch marketed the slave in terms appealing to buyers – and reduced him or her to those qualities. A Gaul lost his cultural identity as a member of this or that tribe to become a potential herdsman; the tall man with a big voice became a potential plowman; the man with broad shoulders a future vineyard worker; and the Briton useless for anything but physical labor. In Horace's sales pitch, the boy's biography – his parents, siblings, and friends, the landscape of home all – disappear with the exception of an instance of hiding out from the whip. The seller shapes the boy's life and abilities to fit the imagined desires of a buyer: even the songs the boy can sing become pleasurable accompaniment to a master's drinking party. The Mesopotamian boy in the sales contract quoted above, too, was "wet clay": reduced to his age, origin, and health, he was Abbas, Eutychus, or "by whatever other name he is called."

The degree to which the slaves on the *catasta* understood their reduction to a set of characteristics useful to buyers but divorced from their own lives depended on the degree to which they had acquired Latin, by origin (Italian birth) or by picking up words and phrases from captors, slave dealers, agents, or even other slaves. The Romans thought that slaves began to learn Latin in the slave market and continued their instruction in their new households (Gellius, *Attic Nights* 4.1.6; Varro, *The Latin Language* 8.6). The law assumes that even slaves who were not newly enslaved might not understand Latin (*Digest* 21.1.65.2). For those with little or no Latin, the marketplace was a noisy scene in which they were the object of meaningless words, intrusive stares, and physical invasion. Men, women, and children who understood Latin heard their lives reduced to a laundry list of useful qualities and divorced from their own pasts, relationships, and purposes.

Historians lack the evidence for how and if slaves in Rome participated in their own sales. It is evident, at least, that they were not completely mute. Given buyers' distrust in the slave dealer's representation of his goods, slaves would have had to speak for potential

buyers: how else could buyers be sure that the slave spoke with difficulty or gutturally, raved, rambled, stammered, or lisped? In addition,
an epitaph from the city of Rome shows that slaves themselves spoke
with each other in the marketplace:

> To Aulus Memmius Clarus. Aulus Memmius Urbanus to his
> fellow freedman and his dearest companion. I do not remem-
> ber, my most virtuous fellow freedman, that there was ever any
> quarrel between you and me. By this epitaph, I call on the gods
> above and the gods below as witnesses that I met you in the
> slave market, that we were made free men together in the same
> household, and that nothing ever separated us except the day of
> your death. (*Corpus of Latin Inscriptions* 6.22355A)

Urbanus's words to Clarus, his fellow ex-slave and beloved companion, reveal something totally outside the purview of sellers and buyers.
Even in the midst of the dealer's manipulation, the noise of the market,
and the intrusive gazes and examinations of buyers, slaves made social
connections with each other. In the case of Clarus and Urbanus, the
market meant the beginning of a long and treasured relationship that
continued through their service as slaves in the same household into
their lives as free men, ending only with the death of Clarus.

An answer to the question of whether Urbanus and Clarus, or any
slave, met their new owners' fantasies of their skills, abilities, and proposed usage was postponed until their arrival at the owner's household
or farm. It is clear that some never made it that far and other failed mis-
erably – from the point of view of their new owners. The geographer
Strabo, writing during the reigns of Augustus and Tiberius, observed
that the large number of people that the Romans seized in Corsica
were useless as slaves: "you can at Rome see, and marvel at, the extent
to which the nature of wild beasts, as also of battening cattle, is mani-
fested in them; for either they cannot endure to live in captivity, or if
they live, they so irritate their purchasers by their apathy and insensi-
bility, that, even although the purchasers may have paid for them no

more than an insignificant sum, nevertheless they repent the purchase" (*Geography* 5.224). For Strabo, the Corsicans' failure to move from captives to slaves stems from bestiality; we might see it as resistance to the process of enslavement and the sale of slaves at Rome or as an example of the depression and misery that the Edict of the Aediles views as a mental defect.

CHAPTER 4

THE PRACTICES OF
SLAVEHOLDERS AND
THE LIVES OF SLAVES

Now I turn to the means by which land is tilled. Some divide these into two parts: men, and those aids to men ... ; others into three: the class of instruments which is articulate, the inarticulate, and the mute; the articulate comprising slaves, the inarticulate comprising cattle, and the mute comprising vehicles. (Varro, *On Agriculture* 1.17.1, trans. W. D. Hooper and H. B. Ash, *LCL*)

I have been much distressed by illness among [my people], the deaths, too, of some of the younger men. Two facts console me somewhat ... : I am always ready to grant my slaves their freedom, so I don't feel their death is so untimely when they die free men, and I allow even those who remain slaves to make a sort of will which I treat as legally binding. ...They can distribute their possessions and make any gifts and bequests they like, within the limits of the household: for the household provides slaves with a country and a sort of citizenship. (Pliny, *Letters* 8.16.1–3, trans. B. Radice, *LCL*)

Iucundus, slave of Taurus, litter bearer.
As long as he lived, he was a man and acted on behalf of himself
    and others.
As long as he lived, he lived honorably.
Callista and Philologus dedicated (this).

                    (*Corpus of Latin Inscriptions* 6.6308, Rome)

Varro, the scholar and writer of the late first century BCE, and Pliny, politician, orator, and imperial governor of the late first and early second centuries CE, each articulate visions of masters and slaves.

Citing a common opinion, Varro defines slaves as tools that speak (*instrumentum vocale*) compared to incomprehensible animals and mute objects. Later in his agricultural manual, he recommends to the slaveholder practices that assume these articulate tools are human beings whose feelings, desires, and perceptions must be taken into account – if their owner is to get the most work out of them. Thus, for Varro, dealing with slaves as human makes them better tools. At first glance, Pliny seems to think of his slaves as human beings rather than as tools: he grieves for his sick slaves, and freeing some of his dying slaves consoles him. Indeed, in other letters Pliny sees himself as a kind master and a father to his slaves, treating them mildly and even indulgently (*Letters* 1.4, 5.19.1). For him, the household is a state, its slaves citizens in it; thus he grants his slaves the privilege of making a will whose terms he honors, as long as they leave their goods to his other slaves and freed slaves. Yet however kind and feeling Pliny may seem, his letter is less concerned with the slaves themselves and their humanity, and more concerned with his own grief: his grants of freedom and wills comfort him. How his slaves felt, he does not say.

If Varro and Pliny speak about the owner's treatment of slaves, the epitaph of Iucundus speaks about the life of a slave who was the object of that treatment (see Figure 44a). In this epitaph from the *columbarium* reserved for the slaves and freed slaves of the wealthy and noble Statilii Tauri, Iucundus's fellow slaves describe the life of Varro's "articulate tool." At first glance, his name, Iucundus, which means agreeable, and his occupational title, litter bearer, seem to mark an acceptance of his condition as a slave: literally, we, and perhaps his noble master Taurus, could read "[the] 'Agreeable,' slave of Taurus, carrier of his litter." However, the epitaph appears in a tomb in which other slaves and freed slaves in the household were buried, many of whom, like Iucundus, named their jobs, including other litter bearers, to whom Iucundus's two commemorators, Callista and Philologus, were tied (see Figure 44b). Other slaves and ex-slaves, then, were the audience for the assertions on Iucundus's epitaph that, while hardly revolutionary, voice a refusal to take everything dished out to him and his.

According to his slave commemorators, he was a man, who defended himself and others, a man who, despite the denigration associated with slavery, lived honorably. Callista and Philologus ignore Pliny's terms of state and citizenship to emphasize a manhood connected with the protection of others and honor.

This chapter looks at the treatment of slaves by slaveholders like Pliny and Varro and the lives of slaves like Iucundus. Slaveholders' practices and enslaved lives, in fact, were not distinct. Slave owners determined the context and conditions in which slaves could and did shape lives for themselves. However, for clarity it seems useful to consider the practices of Roman slaveholders and the lives of slaves separately. The chapter begins with the views of Roman slaveholders, since their treatment of slaves was entwined with their assumptions about slave character, their own desire for loyalty and obedience, and their fears about slaves' motives. All this helps to make sense of slaveholders' use of violence and their grants of favors and privileges. When we turn to slave lives, we must make our way through a crowd of different, individual men and women in a wide variety of situations and occupations. This crowd, however, had in common many of the facts of daily life – such as food, clothing, shelter, and family life, and social relations among slaves. Most slaves, too, lived under the shadow of constant uncertainty; the fear of being sold was a fear that the lowliest farm worker and the comfortable privileged imperial bureaucrat shared. Slavery, after all, was not just a state of being but also a power relationship, defined by the extremity of the power of the slave owner over the slave as well as the slave's powerlessness. Historians have asked whether the enslaved were wholly powerless. The question of accommodation and resistance has been a thorny one: In their daily lives, did slaves consent to their condition and submit to their owners, or did they contend with them? These, then, are the main concerns of this chapter: slaveholders' treatment of slaves and the complex responses of the enslaved.

Three warnings are in order when we look at the lives of slaves. First, as Iucundus's epitaph indicates, the sources do not always offer a direct response to the slaveholder's perceptions and practices: often what we glimpse are other concerns and terms that do not always line up with the slaveholder's. Second, in considering the practices of owners and the lives of slaves, we often set articulate literary and legal texts against less articulate epitaphs. Third, the lives of enslaved men and women can often be seen only through the veil of their owners' words. Slaveholders may observe slave actions accurately enough, but in naming these actions, they make claims that should not be taken as absolute facts. Complaints about slave "laziness," for example, may well observe that slaves did not work as hard or as quickly as their owners wanted. However, by naming the behavior "laziness," they claim slaves' failures and moral inadequacy. In fact, the behavior may reflect acts of resistance or slaves' attempts to control the practice and pace of their own labor.

Roman Slaveholders Look at Their Slaves: The "Good" Slave and the "Bad"

Roman lawyers, authors, politicians, and emperors express a variety of opinions about "good" slaves and "bad." As described in the discussion of buyers in the slave market, the Edict of the Aediles depicts the good slave as loyal, obedient, diligent, vigilant, thrifty, upright, and hardworking. In other words, in the view of Roman slaveholders, good slaves did their work with attention and care, followed orders, and did not cheat or waste their owners' resources (which included slaves' own time). In the late third and early second centuries BCE, the comic poet Plautus put loyal slaves (as well as his more famous slave tricksters) on stage to entertain an audience that included slaves as well as Roman citizens. The self-conscious claims of these characters gave the audience a humorous version of what pleased slaveholders. Plautus's good slave follows orders quickly, without dawdling or back talk; he does not sleep on the job; he looks after his owner's interests, whether the master is present or absent; his master's interests become his own;

he anticipates not only his master's orders but also his desires and even his moods; he has a healthy sense of fear and self-preservation.

Here and in other texts, good slaves are not merely things but also human beings: in fact, it is their most human characteristics – speech, will, and desire – that ideally line up with their owner's. In effect, for Roman slaveholders, loyalty meant slaves acted to fulfill slaveholders' ends; slaves' words expressed their submission to their owners' will; and slaves wanted what their owners desired. However, Plautus's good slaves make clear what later authors comment on – that fear of punishment especially produces this sort of slave service and loyalty. Messenio, a slave in Plautus's *Menaechmi,* spells out the duty of servile loyalty and the cost of laziness: whippings, fetters, and condemnation to working in a mill where the slave will be fatigued, hungry, and cold. He then explains to the audience:

> 'Cause I'm way more happy to put up with words than whips – I hate 'em,
> and I like to eat grits way more than I want to grind 'em.
> That's why I snap to my boss's orders, I follow 'em meek and mild,
> And it does me a lot of good.
>
> (977–981, trans. A. Richlin)

If slaveholders worried that only punishment kept the slave in line, they had cause to doubt even the motives of the good slave. This doubt had some relief in repeated tales of slaves who sacrificed their lives for their owners or endured pain to save them. These stories take place during the civil wars of the Republic or under tyrannical emperors in the Principate, when the social order did not uphold the slaveholder's power and when the slaveholder him- or herself was threatened with death, violence, or dishonor. In other words, the stories show slaves acting loyally when they themselves were not threatened with punishment. Some killed their owners at their request – and then usually killed themselves – to save their owners from their enemies; some put on their owners' clothes to be killed in their place; some hid their owners. Still others, like the slave of the orator Marcus Antonius, endured torture but did not inform on their masters. As Valerius Maximus, the first-century author of *Memorable Deeds and Sayings,* tells the story (6.8.1), Antonius was accused of a sexual crime, and his prosecutors demanded that a particular slave (Valerius does not name him) undergo interrogation because he supposedly carried a lantern for Antonius when he went out to commit the deed. Standing among the spectators at the trial, the slave realized that the demand meant his own torture (since slave testimony was always taken under torture). However, he did not flee, and when he returned home with his master, he urged his master to turn him over for examination and torture. This was his own choice, for his master, thinking of his slave's welfare, resisted. Promising his master he would say nothing to harm his case, the slave convinced his master. He kept his word and endured a whipping, the rack, and burning.

Such stories became noteworthy because, as Valerius Maximus observes, the loyalty of slaves was "less expected." In the common perception of slaveholders, most slaves were bad slaves. In its discussion of slave defects and flaws, the Edict of the Aediles outlines the qualities buyers sought to avoid. It presents masters' visions of the bad slave, which includes complaints and charges repeated in a wide variety of literary sources. Bad slaves cannot or will not control their bodies: they are greedy and oversexed; they love to stuff themselves with food and get drunk. They disobey or cause trouble within the household: they are quick-tempered, obstinate, impudent, reckless, fickle, and quarrelsome. Or they are mentally unstable: some are mad or have periods of unreason, others are just silly, and still others are superstitious or religious fanatics. Many complaints focus on work: bad slaves are lazy, idle, and tardy; some waste time; others fail to do their jobs. Wandering and truancy are common complaints. Bad slaves waste resources, especially their owners': some are frivolous, some gamble, and above all, slaveholders charge, slaves steal – presumably because they are both greedy and dishonest.

These accusations have a pattern. In various ways, bad slaves are not subject to their owner's will. Quite the reverse, in various ways they act for themselves. They try to do what they want to do, and since, in the common opinion of slaveholders, they are dominated by their own bodily appetites, this often means physical excess. Far from being effective tools, they do not do their work, or they do it poorly, and, instead of producing, they consume what belongs to the slaveholder. Slave runaways, a virtual obsession in law, combine all these elements. The runaway dramatically demonstrates an independence of will, disloyalty, lack of devotion, and bad service. Importantly, too, he is guilty of stealing the slave owner's property – himself!

At the extreme, slaveholders saw their slaves as enemies capable of violence against them. A Roman proverb captures this anxiety: "You have as many enemies as you have slaves." It is difficult to estimate the actual frequency of slaves' assaults on their owners. After the three major slave revolts between 135 and 70 BCE, the sources report only smaller disturbances and, most often, attacks on individual slave owners. Accounts of these attacks see them not as discrete events but as evidence of a general servile criminality. The historian Tacitus, for example, recounts the murder of Pedanius Secundus, prefect of the city of Rome, in 61 CE by one of his slaves (*Annals* 14.42–45). Afterwards, when the senate debated whether to uphold the ancient custom that required the execution of all the other slaves living under the same roof, Tacitus portrays the senator Gaius Cassius warning his fellow senators about the natural temperament of slaves: "Now that our households comprise nations, with customs the reverse of our own, with foreign cults or with none, you will never coerce such a medley of humanity except by terror" (14.44). Likewise, when Pliny the Younger tells the story of the murder of Larcius Macedo by his slaves, he bemoans the dangers that all masters must fear from their slaves. Although Macedo was a bad master, proud and cruel in Pliny's judgment, Pliny himself claims that even a mild and kind master cannot feel safe in a world where slaves' criminality, not their rationality, explains the murder of masters (*Letters* 3.14.1; 3.14.5).

The Practices of Roman Slaveholders

Slave owners' expectations, desires, and fears shaped their treatment of slaves, and more generally, the practice of mastery. On the one hand, slaveholders reacted to particular situations, and their behavior was a matter of their own desires and their common sense about slaves' character – that is, the views discussed above. On the other hand, as pointed out in Chapter 2, as a large-scale slave system was established in Rome, Roman practices of dealing with slaves and extracting their labor and cooperation became more self-conscious and more polished. By the first century CE, some slaveholders advocated a fatherly kindness in the relations of master and slave – often termed benevolent paternalism.

Through the entire history of slavery at Rome, however, physical restraint and violence lay at the center of slaveholders' practices. Owners, in other words, exercised the power that they held over the bodies of their human property, and they exercised it fully. So common was their belief that punishment kept slaves in line that early on, as noted above, it became a joke in comedy. Slaveholders chained recalcitrant slaves and runaways, using a variety of manacles, fetters, and neck chains. The use of leg fetters, like those in Figure 34, allowed the slave some movement and the use of his hands and arms for work, so the slave owner could prevent fights or trouble while retaining the slave's use value. In his agricultural manual, Columella recommends this sort of containment for vineyard workers whose job required mental sharpness, apparently because, in the slaveholder's logic, the smart slave was a troublesome slave (1.9.4). Chained slaves in the country were housed in *ergastula* (slave prisons): ideally, according to Columella, the prison had narrow windows to emit light, placed high enough so that the slaves could not reach them with their hands (1.6.3).

Troublesome slaves were marked on their faces with brands or, more likely, tattoos to identify them and the "crimes" for which they had been marked. When caught, some slaves had metal collars riveted around their necks: the collar had an engraving that identified the slave as a fugitive and often requested his return to his owner. The tag on the

34. Leg fetters. (Photo Rheinisches Landesmuseum,Trier)

35. Slave collar with *bulla* (tag). (su concessione del Minstero per i Beni e le Attività Culturali – Soprintendenza Speciale per i Beni Archeologici di Roma)

collar from Rome, depicted in Figure 35, reads: "I have run away: hold on to me. When you return me to my master Zoninus, you will get a gold *solidus*" (*Selected Latin Inscriptions* 8731). The use of these collars was common enough that the message could be abbreviated "TMQF" (*Tene me quia fugio*) – Hold on to me since I flee (*Selected Latin Inscriptions* 9454).

Slaveholders could send troublesome slaves to work in a flour mill. This punishment was common enough by the late third and early second centuries BCE that Plautus made humor out of the slaves' fear of the hunger, cold, and fatigue suffered by those sentenced to work in a mill (see above). Much later, in his second century CE novel the *Metamorphoses,* Apuleius describes the condition of slaves in a mill:

Their skin was black and blue with scars from whippings; their scarred backs were crusted rather than clothed with patched rags; some had no more covering than a bit of cloth; and all wore garments so tattered that their bodies were visible through the tears. Their foreheads were tattooed; their heads were half shaved; irons clanked on their feet; their faces were sallow and ugly; the smoky gloom of the reeking overheated room had clouded and dulled their eyes; and, like boxers who are covered with sand when they fight in the arena, their bodies were a dirty white from the flour. (9.12, trans. J. Lindsay with changes)

In the Republic, slaveholders could condemn a slave to death by crucifixion, burning, or having him thrown into the arena to face wild animals. They could also have a slave tortured by various means – burning, racking, and flogging – and, in fact, they could purchase the services of torturers. In the city of Puteoli, a company of undertakers tortured and executed slaves for private individuals and state officials. An inscription sets out the regulations for services and the provision of equipment. Its dispassionate language about equipment describes what some slaves endured:

If anyone wishes to have a slave – male or female – punished privately, he who wishes to have the punishment inflicted shall do so as follows. If he wants to put the slave on the cross or fork, the contractor must supply the posts, chains, ropes for floggers and the floggers themselves. The person having the punishment inflicted is to pay 4 sesterces for each of the operatives who carry the fork, and the same for floggers and for the executioner.

The magistrate shall give orders for such punishments as he exacts in his public capacity, and when orders are given (the contractor) is to be ready to exact the punishment. He is to set up crosses and supply without charge nails, pitch, wax, tapers, and anything else that is necessary for this in order to deal with the condemned man. (*L'Année épigraphique* 1971, no. 88, trans. J. F. Gardner and T. Wiedemann)

The public administration of the dire punishments of crucifixion, burning, condemnation to the arena, and torture, like Crassus's crucifixion of Spartacus's followers along the Via Appia in 70 BCE, put on spectacles of what happened to disobedient slaves. Even more, such spectacles displayed the vulnerability of slaves to the society as a whole.

In the Principate, there was increasing regulation of slave owners' use of such punishments. They were not entirely banned; rather, the state stepped into the place of the owner to determine if and when they were to be administered. Moreover, slave testimony continued to be taken under torture. Although Roman lawyers and writers were well aware that under torture the slave might say anything to stop the pain, the realization did not change the practice or the belief that only physical pain would extract the truth from the slave (*Digest* 48.18.1.23). Not only were slaves viewed as liars: their condition of enslavement made any and all servile words suspect to their owners. In their view, the slave, motivated by fear of the slave owner's power to punish, tried to please by word and deed because he or she had to, and every enslaved response smacked of duplicity and was suspected by the slaveholder. Thus, the institution of slavery that gave slave owners physical power over their slaves and made slaves the tools of their owners shaped slaveholders' perceptions of slave character and in turn mandated physical abuse as a practice for getting the truth out of an enslaved person, defined by the institution itself as untruthful.

Whipping or beating slaves was so much a matter of common sense that it is a joke in comedy, a line in poetry, a scene in novels, or a phrase in philosophical tracts. In literature, slaves get beaten for failing to do their jobs. The poet Martial asks rhetorically if he needs a reason to punish his cook other than a badly cooked dinner (8.23). We hear of hairdressers hit for curls out of place and waiters whipped for clumsiness. In other scenarios, muttering, loudness, defiant looks, and even coughs and sneezes incite a flogging, beating, or shackles. Sometimes slaveholders took their frustrations or bad moods out on their slaves – or so say Roman writers. In the second century CE, the doctor Galen reports that angry slave owners punched their slaves in the mouth, kicked them, gouged out their eyes, and stabbed them with a pen if they had one in hand (*Diseases of the Mind* 4). Galen takes to task owners who punched their slaves, not for the injury done to the slave but for the bruises owners inflict on their own hands; he recommends these slaveholders control their anger, wait, and later direct someone else to beat or whip the offending slave. Like Galen, many authors criticize the physical punishment of slaves as failures of the slaveholder's self-control, temper, or social grace, but no Roman author or lawyer ever denies the slave owner's power to punish his or her slave. Indeed, the emphasis on *the slaveholder's* self-control makes clear the vulnerability of every slave whose body belonged to another.

This attitude is part of a self-conscious practice of mastery that developed over the history of the slave system at Rome. Although the agricultural manuals of Cato, Varro, and Columella focus on rural slaves, they spell out elements in this development that affected all slaves. Rural slaveholders wanted to get as much work out of their slaves as possible, and their calculations of jobs and time became more detailed and complex. Slave owners are urged to match jobs to body type and to character (see the earlier discussion) and to distinguish clearly the tasks assigned to specific slaves and to organize workers in squads (Columella 1.9.7). The latter was supposed to make slaves work effectively and, at the same time, pacify them (Columella 11.1.27). The agriculture writers worried about servile laziness and loitering, and their instructions on the slave manager and his wife (*vilicus* and *vilica*) and the owner's control of the pair became more elaborate and moralistic – a quality that applies to their attempts to control slaves in general.

All of the agricultural writers assume what we can see in law – that the slave owner should provide for the basic needs of the body – food, clothing, and housing (*Digest* 34.1.6). What this meant for slave bodies is explored later. For the moment, the issue is how the agricultural manuals depict treatment where the physical needs of slaves are concerned. All adopt an instrumental attitude: food, clothing, and shelter are ends to keep slaves at their work. They acknowledge that slaves cannot work if they are hungry or cold (Cato, *On Agriculture* 5.2), and, Cato, for one, calculates the amount of food handed out by the physical labor done by the slave (see below). The standard for clothing is utility (Columella 11.1.21): it should ward off cold and rain, so that no weather inhibits working outside (1.8.9). Moreover, food, extra clothing, time off, and permission to graze cattle for slaves' own uses serve as incentives to make slaves more diligent at work (Varro 1.17.7).

The agricultural writers, who make detailed observations about food and clothing, do not discuss slave housing itself but mention it only in passing: slave rooms, a resting room for slaves, the kitchen, quarters for the slave manager (*vilicus*), and the *ergastulum* for the chained slaves. In fact, it seems that the agricultural writers describe the buildings on farms and vineyards in terms of their own interests in effective production: slave quarters are subordinate to this concern, except where control and containment are the issues. The manager's quarters should be positioned for the best surveillance of the slaves in his charge (Varro 1.13.2; Columella 1.6.7), and slaves should be housed as close to each other as possible to make the duties of keeping track of them easier for the manager (Columella 1.6.8).

Family life and social life do not figure as basic needs of slaves in the treatment of slaves prescribed in the agricultural manuals. Like housing, slaves' social relations and families are mentioned in passing or as a subordinate topic to a larger concern on the slaveholder's mind. We get a glimpse of slaves' social relations in references to holidays, the slave owner's concern with order, and the manager's duty to keep peace among the slaves. In general, owners were concerned with control, so, for example, the manual writers refer to social situations, all of which involve disorder or tensions – adjudicating quarrels, avenging the injured, and punishing those who incite revolt (Columella 1.8.18; Varro 1.17.5).

Legally, slaves could not marry or claim their children or any other familial relations. In fact, they did marry, and a variety of literary sources refer to slave spouses, children, parents, and siblings – sometimes with a degree of sentimentality (Martial 4.13; Juvenal 11.146 ff.). Roman lawyers often talk about slave familial relationships, although they are usually concerned with slave mothers because the owner of a slave mother also owned her children. The latter part of the chapter examines the conditions of the slave family. The concern here is the limited attention paid to the slave families in the agricultural manuals, again, usually in the context of social control.

In general, owners were interested in the sexual needs of male slaves. According to his biographer, Cato allowed slaves to have sexual relations, but as a release for enslaved men and in a way that profited Cato: "Since he thought that what made slaves most troublesome was their sexual needs, he allowed them to get together with the female slaves for a fixed price" (Plutarch, *Life of Cato* 21.2). The needs, even imagined, of enslaved women did not enter into these considerations, and the use of slave women to control slave men was simply assumed. The manuals focus especially on foremen and managers: a slave manager who has sex on his mind will not pay attention to his job (Columella 11.1.14). A woman, a fellow slave, will keep him in control and help him manage the farm and other slaves (Columella 1.8.5); a wife and children, too, make foremen more reliable and attached to the farm (Varro 1.17.5).

Varro, for example, does not mention other slaves, except for the herdsmen whose women, too, keep them bound to the place. Varro talks about the relations of these men and women as the "human breeding of herdsmen" (2.10.6) and, immediately before this discussion, gives instructions on the breeding and care of dogs and mules. In his logic, slave herders, male and female, belong to a more general topic he calls "mules, dogs, and herdsmen." Roman slaveholders were aware that slave family relations – or perhaps in their terms breeding, enlarged their own property. Columella exempts women who have raised three children from labor, and he frees those who have raised four (1.8.19). However, his concern is reproduction, not the relations within a slave family: he does not mention the father or the relations of parents and children.

The manuals reveal one more aspect of treatment – what we might call a psychological dimension. Slaveholders tried to affect the mind and spirit of their slaves. Even Cato advises that the slave manager (*vilicus*) should know the mind of the slaves in his charge (5.5). By the late first century, the manuals urge the use of words, not whips, when words attain the same ends (Varro 1.17.5). Varro recommends consulting rural slaves on the work that the master wants done, for "they will be less inclined to think that they are looked down upon, and rather ... that they are held in some esteem by the master" (1.17.6). Columella explains that he talks to his slaves about new projects, "as if they were more experienced." *He* studies their abilities and intelligence, and *they,* in their master's view, become "more willing to set about a piece of work on which they think that their opinions have been asked and their advice followed" (1.8.15).

To us, the acknowledgment of slave consciousness in the manuals may seem feigned. Perhaps, again, it is merely another example of the instrumental approach to mastery. Treating slaves as if they had ideas produces more work and better cooperation. In other authors, we can see an ideal of mastery that insists on the slave's humanity and proclaims the importance of slaveholders' kindness. This practice of mastery – benevolent paternalism – is articulated most eloquently by Seneca, the philosopher, politician, and tutor of the emperor Nero.

In a famous letter on master–slave relations (*Letters* 47), Seneca urges the friendly treatment of slaves as opposed to what he claims is the common practice that deals with them as draft animals, looks on them with disdain, and inspires fear by the use of the whip. Against owners who claim "they are slaves," Seneca answers that they are human beings (*homines*), housemates (*contubernales*), humble friends (*humiles amici*), and ultimately fellow slaves (*conservi*) (47.1). For Seneca, they are fellow slaves because every man is a "slave" to something or someone – fear, lust, greed, ambition, a rich wife, a lover. He praises the use of verbal punishments in place of the whip and suggests that slaveholders invite deserving slaves to the table, even the lowly mule driver or plowman: masters should evaluate slaves by their character, not their occupation (47.13, 15). Our Roman ancestors, Seneca claims, acted this way, and the master incurred no ill will and the slave felt no insult.

In these good old days, the master was called father of the household and slaves members of the household. Seneca urges that slaves should revere, not fear, their master.

Seneca does not advocate the abolition of slavery but a paternalism that strengthens the institution of slavery itself. Whatever moral quality slaves might attain and however human they are, Seneca sees slaves as inferiors who can never rise above the level of humble friends. Seneca's vocabulary makes it clear that he expects obedience and respect as the master – based on a reverence that compels the slave to obey because it is the right thing to do, not because of the whip. Nor does Seneca question the common view that slaves should please their owners. Moreover, he covers over slave owners' reliance on the labor of their slaves by defining slaves as dependent. Like Pliny, whose description of his slaves' privilege of making a will imagines that he is the care-taker and his slaves the cared for, Seneca sees slaves as a burden to their owner who must feed and clothe them, watch that they do not steal, and use their services (*The Tranquility of the Mind* 8.8).

Paternalism had as much or more to do with masters as with slaves. Upper-class authors recommend kindness and care in works addressed to other upper-class slaveholders, and master–slave relations serve the elite as a way of talking about themselves. For Seneca, the relations of master and slave serve as a metaphor for thinking about unequal power relations in general and for the relations of senators and emperors in particular. For Pliny, as discussed at the beginning of this chapter, mas-terly benevolence belongs to a portrait that he fashions of himself for his upper-class readers.

How and if paternalism translated into practice – better living con-ditions and greater privileges – is a more difficult question. If Seneca and Pliny practiced what they preached, we can assume that civility and patience characterized the slave owner's orders and comments to slaves. Pliny claims the slaves at his Laurentine villa had living quar-ters good enough for his guests. Neither Pliny nor Seneca mentions slave families. When Pliny thinks of his generosity in allowing slaves to make wills, he never goes so far as to alienate slaves' property that, legally, belongs to him. All slave gifts, bequests, and distributions circulate within his own household; outside that household, his slaves can give nothing to a husband, wife, sister, brother, child, or friend. For Pliny, these relations matter less than his definition of the household as a *res publica:* his vision of slaves' "citizenship" in the "republic" of the household ignores slaves' own emphasis on family, friendships, and relations among their peers (see below).

Perhaps Pliny refers to his slaves' *peculia,* but he does not pointedly acknowledge this privilege, known from other sources, in his concern to depict his own masterly generosity. The *peculium* was property granted specifically by the owner for the slave's uses: it could include cash, real estate, tools, livestock, clothing, food, and even slaves. In the words of the jurist Florentinus, "a *peculium* is made up of anything a slave has been able to save by his own economies or has been given by a third party in return for meritorious services or has been allowed by his master to keep as his own" (*Digest* 15.1.39). Slaves in commerce used their *peculia* to generate income for their owners. Ultimately, the *peculium* belonged to the slave owner, who could withdraw the privilege that he or she had granted. However, it is clear that slaves with *peculia* also accumulated funds for their own uses – whether that meant buying their freedom, purchasing a tombstone, acquiring food or clothes, or paying for visits to prostitutes. Slaveholders may have seen their grant of a *peculium* as an act of kindness or generosity; yet, at the same time, the privilege had tangible benefits for slave owners that they themselves acknowledged: commercial income earned by the slave, a more diligent performance of duties, or even the price paid for the slave's freedom.

Whether paternalism translated into the greatest of masterly favors, manumission, is equally an open question. Although Pliny mentions his freedmen, and we know that he freed many of his slaves, his only mention of manumission in the context of paternalism comes when he describes the grant of freedom to dying slaves (8.16). From other sources, we learn that the promise of freedom was held out as a reward for good behavior, loyalty, and service. Some slave owners freed slaves by provisions in their wills and told the fortunate slaves of this promised end of their servitude – an inducement, if not a guarantee, of their submission to their owners for their lifetimes. Moreover, as discussed in Chapter 2, former owners had a claim to their ex-slaves' compliance, respect, and labor.

The frequency of manumission is important for understanding the Roman practice of mastery because the possibility of freedom holds out a promise to the slave, which the owner could use to secure the slave's acceptance of his or her condition as one that had an end. Most historians believe that the Romans manumitted many slaves and often. Certainly, manumission was a common practice in Roman society, and a variety of sources indicate that there were many freed slaves in Roman society. Yet generalizations about the generosity of Roman slaveholders and the assumptions of their slaves require care. First, we have no firm statistics for the frequency of manumission. Second, variations of location and occupation – not to mention the particular practices of individual slave owners – shaped slaves' opportunities for manumission. As far as we can determine, rural slaves, except for the female slaves in Columella who gained freedom after the birth of four children, could not expect their freedom, nor could urban slaves in lowly positions. Thus, although there were many freed slaves in Roman society, and although certain slaves had a firm expectation of manumission, it was probably the case that most slaves lived without a prospect of freedom. For those who did, the slave owner's power to grant freedom worked to his or her advantage.

The Lives of Slaves

No Roman slave tells us what it was like to live under these practices of mastery, but we can glimpse what such practices meant for the daily lives of slaves. The crowd of slaves included countless different life stories and complex differences among the enslaved. Slaves' lives were affected by gender and occupation; the type of household to which they belonged; the wealth, character, and philosophy of the master;

and, of course, the personality and history of the individual slave man, woman, and child. How these factors combined and interacted with one another, too, determined the life of each enslaved person. A comparison of the epitaph of Iucundus, the litter bearer of Taurus, discussed at the beginning of this chapter, with that of Musicus Scurranus, slave of the emperor Tiberius and treasurer in the imperial administration of the province of Lugdunensis in ancient Gaul, suggests the wide variation of slave lives:

> To Musicus Scurranus, slave of the emperor Tiberius Caesar Augustus, treasurer at the treasury of Gaul in the province of Lugdunensis, a well-deserving man, from his slaves who were with him in Rome when he died: Venustus, business agent; Decimianus, household treasurer; Dicaeus, secretary; Mutatus, secretary; Creticus, secretary; Agathopus, doctor; Epaphra, silver caretaker; Primio, caretaker of clothing; Communis, bedchamber servant; Pothus, attendant; Tiasus, cook; Facilis, attendant; Anthus, silver caretaker; Hedylus, bedchamber servant; Firmus, cook; Secunda (*Corpus of Latin Inscriptions* 6.5197, Rome)

An agent of the emperor in the imperial bureaucracy, Musicus held a privileged position in the world of slaves. As his epitaph makes clear, he had his own slaves, sixteen of whom were with him when he died in Rome. These slaves included secretaries who helped in his work and domestic servants whose job titles indicate that Musicus not only had his own establishment but also lived a life of comfort and even luxury. Agathopus attended to his health; Epaphra and Anthus took care of his silver, Primio his clothing; Pothus, Facilis, Communis, and Hedylus waited on him; and Firmus and Tiasus prepared his meals.

The following discussion focuses on the lives of ordinary slaves, not the Musicuses of Roman society, who led lives more comfortable than poor freeborn Romans. Even so, it is useful to remember that despite his post in the imperial bureaucracy, his wealth, and his comfortable life, Musicus, like any slave, was disdained as a person without honor by the freeborn and subject to the power of an owner who could sell him or beat him. After considering the basic facts of slave life – food, clothing, and housing, the chapter turns to the possibilities of family life. Finally, it takes up the question of how slaves lived under the basic condition of every slave – the violence that lay at the heart of slaveholders' practice and their desire for slaves whose wills matched their own needs.

Although all the agricultural writers cover the distribution of food, only Cato notes specific amounts, determined by season and physical labor. Ordinary workers should be given four *modii* of wheat per month in the winter, and four and a half in the summer. The manager (*vilicus*), his wife and assistant (*vilica*), the overseer (*epitata*), and the herdsman (*opilio*) get three, presumably because they did less physical labor. Chained slaves were given four pounds of bread in the winter, and five when they began to work on the vines – to be reduced to four when the figs ripened. The distinction between grain and bread must relate to slaves' ability to prepare gruel or bread from the grain – difficult for chained slaves in the *ergastulum*. Later, Columella talks as if the staff under the direction of the *vilica* prepared bread and gruel. By the mid-first century, the standard was five *modii* of grain per month (and some cash; Seneca, *Moral Letters* 80.7), a ration that translates into 3,000–3,500 calories per day. In addition to grain or bread, slaves got low-quality wine – for Cato's slaves, ten quadrantals per year and extra on the holidays of the Saturnalia and the Compitalia. This diet was topped off with one *modius* of salt per year, oil, and a relish made of olives.

This high-carbohydrate diet fueled workers but lacked protein and certain vitamins derived from green vegetables and fruit. In the country, rations of bread, wine, and olive relish could be supplemented by vegetables, greens, and fruit, cultivated and wild, and by the livestock that Varro says slaves kept for themselves – although animals reserved for slave use were a boon granted by the slave owner. In the city, too, urban households sometimes had vegetable gardens. Apparently, domestic servants ate the leftovers of their owners' dinner parties, and some owners themselves divided the leftovers among their domestic staff. Some slaves must have supplemented this diet with food cadged in the kitchen or on its way to the table.

The basic dress of most slaves was a tunic. Cato recommends a tunic of three and a half feet in length, a blanket, and a pair of sturdy wooden shoes every other year. Old garments, he advises, should be turned in to make patchwork blankets or cloaks for protection against the cold and rain. Typical rustic wear included a cloak of wool or leather, sometimes with a hood (see Figures 36a and b and Figures 48–50). It seems that slaves were distinguished from citizens by the quality of their clothes, not the type. As everyday clothing, Roman citizens, too, wore tunics and cloaks, varying in style and fabric for men and women, rich and poor. Only in formal attire did poor citizens stand out from slaves (Figure 37). All male citizens had the right to wear the toga, decorated to indicate senatorial rank or office. Female citizens wore a *stola* (a long garment worn over the tunic) and a special hair band. In practice, then, most slaves looked like poor Romans – at least when the latter were not wearing togas or *stolae* for some formal occasion. Telling the difference between slave and free was sometimes difficult. Stories about republican politicians or emperors disguising themselves as slaves meant they achieved anonymity by dressing like the poor. Law tried to distinguish free women from slave women by dress. Lewd behavior toward a Roman citizen woman was cause for a suit for injury unless she was wearing slave clothing. Without her *stola* and special hair band, a poor citizen woman who was dressed in a dark tunic of inferior quality would seem to have been as vulnerable as a slave woman.

To some extent, slaves' clothing depended on occupation. Slaves working in a mill wore rags. Mine workers (whether free or slave)

36. (a) Relief of workers digging and hoeing, Arlon, late second–third century CE. (David Colling – Institut Archéologique du Luxembourg) (b) Relief of workers winnowing grain, Mainz. (© Landesmuseum Mainz)

are depicted wearing a tunic and a short apron made of leather strips (Figure 38). In a tomb relief from Trier, four young women, probably slaves, wear ankle boots and calf-length tunics, cinched at the waist, with long sleeves; they attend their older mistress, dressed in the garb of a proper Roman matron with *stola* and *palla* (mantle) (Figure 39). A painting of a drinking party in a house in Pompeii depicts servants attending to the guests (Figure 40). On the far left, a small slave in a simple white tunic removes the shoe of a guests in a white tunic and purple mantle; a taller servant whose tunic has thin purple stripes hands the guest a cup of wine. To the left are two other guests – a man

37. Dress of Roman
citizen men and
women: funerary
relief from the
Via Statilia, Rome,
75–50 BCE.
(Faraglia, Neg.
D-DAI-Rom
1929.01728)

in a green mantle and another in white mantle. He is turned toward a
bald man seated in front of a window. Dressed in a long green garment
whose edge is pulled over his head, the man leans against a small black
boy in a sleeveless red garment – perhaps a special dress for a sexual
favorite or at least a special slave whose color made him an exotic,
luxury object. In front of the tables, a small servant, again dressed in a
white tunic, supports a much larger man in a red mantle as the latter
vomits.

Attendants, servants, and waiters in large wealthy households
might wear fancier fabrics when they served at their owners' table
or accompanied them in public (for the dress of servants, see also

38. Mine workers, Linares, second century CE. (Photo Deutsches Bergbau-Museum, Bochum)

Figures 1–2, 14, and 52–53). Some slave attendants wore a kind of badge on their outfits. In Petronius's first-century novel, the vulgar Trimalchio, himself an ex-slave, has slaves who wear outlandish costumes or expensive outfits. Trimalchio's doorkeeper wears a green tunic with a cherry-red belt; his money manager has evening clothes of Tyrian-dyed fabric worth 10,000 sesterces. These details about slave dress belong to Petronius's jokes about his character Trimalchio: his slaves imitate a master who himself wears ridiculous getups. However, a privileged slave like Musicus Scurranus, whose epitaph is quoted above, had clothes numerous and fancy enough to require a slave caretaker – not unexpected for a man who also had caretakers for his silver objects. For most slaves, however, the simple tunics worn by the enslaved women and men in Figures 39 and 40 were probably the norm (for the clothing of bakers, fullers, salespeople, and craftsmen, see Figures 64, 66, and 70–73).

In general, clothes belonged to the slave's *peculium* only if the slave owner had given them to the slave for "his exclusive and permanent use": however, finer clothing worn only for a "particular purpose or on special occasions, such as attending him as footman or waiting upon

39. Maid servants on a tomb relief, Trier, early third century CE. (Photo Rheinisches Landesmuseum, Trier)

him at dinner" belonged to the master (*Digest* 15.1.25). On a farm like Cato's, even work clothes were in the slaveholder's control: slaves had to turn them in to get new ones, and they themselves could not use the old ones for their own purposes (*On Agriculture* 59).

For most Roman authors, the term for a slave room (*cella*) signals a small, cramped space. Archaeologists have identified small, clustered rooms in rural villas as slave quarters. In a villa at Gragnano (Villa 34), built perhaps in the first century BCE, for example, five small rooms (5–9) on the west side of the main courtyard may have been slave rooms; a staircase (13) led to a second story and probably at least five more rooms (Figure 41). The two courtyards to the south of the main courtyard (c and b on Figure 41), too, are surrounded by small rooms identified as slave quarters. These small rooms measure 3 × 2 meters (10 × 6.5 feet) and have plain, undecorated walls. In courtyard

40. Painting from the House of the Triclinium (V.2.4), Pompeii. (Photo
Michael Larvey su concessione del Minstero per i Beni e le Attività Culturali –
Soprintendenza Speciale per i Beni Archeologici di Napoli e Pompei)

c there were iron stocks with fourteen openings to chain one or both
ankles of slaves, so we have some idea of how this area was used – perhaps some version of an *ergastulum*. How the other rooms were occupied is unknown, but Cato provides a hint in his agricultural manual
when he sets out the equipment for a vineyard of 100 *iugera*. For a
staff of sixteen, he suggests four beds, four mattresses, and four cover-
lets – not to mention one chamber pot (11). Clearly, then, slaves shared

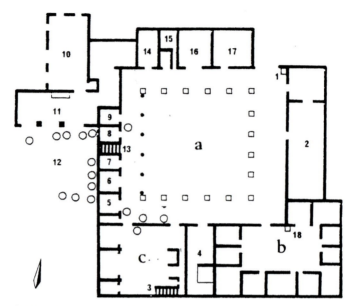

41. Plan of Villa 34, Gragnano. Key: (1) Drinking trough, (2) Cattle shed/
stable, (3) Stairs, (4) Bakery, (5–9) Slave rooms, (10) Pressing room, (11) Storage
area, (12) Storage for earthenware vessels, (13) Stairs, (14–17) Rooms whose
use is uncertain, (18) Oven. (From F. H. Thompson, *The Archaeology of Greek
and Roman Slavery* [London: Gerald Duckworth & Co., 2003], p. 85, fig. 24. By
permission of Gerald Duckworth & Co. Ltd.)

beds and, we should expect, rooms. However, perhaps like the resting
room or kitchen mentioned in the agricultural manuals, courtyard b
at Gragnano provided an open space for work, cooking, eating, and
socializing. Other rural slaves – herdsmen, shepherds, and bird keepers – slept near the animals that they tended (Columella 1.6.8; Varro
2.1.26, 3.9.7).

Some of the grand urban houses of the Roman elite had their own
slave quarters. In Rome, on the northern slope of the Palatine in what
was a neighborhood of the rich and famous in the Republic, archaeologists have found on a semi-subterranean floor what they think are
the quarters of the slaves of Marcus Aemilius Scaurus, whose house
featured an atrium famous for its luxury and huge marble columns
(Figure 42). The thirty small plainly plastered rooms, which may

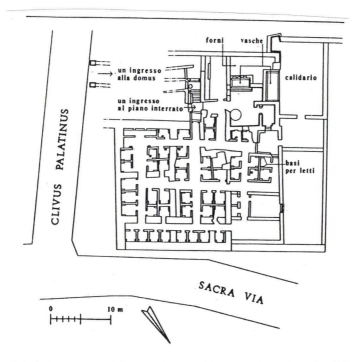

42. Slave quarters on the Palatine, House of Marcus Aemilius Scaurus (?), Rome. (From A. Carandini, *Schiavi in Italia, Gli strumenti pensanti dei Romani fra tarda repubblica e medio impero* [Rome: Nuova Italia Scientifica, 1988])

have occupied the floor below the atrium, are about 1.8 × 1.5 meters and about two meters high; in them are what may have been a base for a bed set against one wall. In some of the houses of the wealthy in Pompeii, slave quarters and the areas devoted to work, like the kitchen, are marginalized to the edges of the owner's living spaces and the most public reception areas of the house. In the House of the Menander, four small rooms of about 3 × 3 meters with plainly plastered walls and small high windows may have been slave quarters (35–38 in Figure 8); a staircase led to similar rooms upstairs. Located near a latrine (39), the stable yard (34), and a stable (29) and opening off a narrow corridor, these rooms seem to squeeze slaves into the peripheral areas of the master's social space. Slave quarters may have been even more cramped than the material remains suggest, for off-hand comments in several Roman sources suggest that these rooms were shared.

Archaeologists have had difficulty in identifying slave rooms. Small, plainly decorated, or undecorated rooms could have served other purposes – storage or stalls for animals. This problem itself is significant. The exchangeability in room usage that characterizes the archaeological record might represent ancient reality. Slaves, like goods and animals, occupied the same marginal space. As the agricultural writers subordinated slave housing to the productive aspects of a farm or villa, houses expressed their owner's wealth and status, to which slaves and their living space were subordinate. In some houses, even large ones, in fact, we cannot find a trace of slave quarters. References in the legal and literary sources suggest that slaves simply slept near their work – the cook in his kitchen, the nurse with her charge, the personal servant at the door of his or her owner's bedroom or at her feet. Others bedded down where they could find a spot.

Slave housing raises questions about slaves' relations with each other, for physical space shaped the social space of slaves and hence their family lives, friendships, and even feuds and rivalries. Perhaps slave social activities took place in open areas of the house – the stable yard in the House of the Menander, the small atrium outside the kitchen in the House of the Vetti at Pompeii (see Figures 6 and 8), and even the peristyles of these houses when owner and guests were elsewhere. At the lavish, aristocratic villa of Oplontis on the Bay of Naples, what has been identified as a service courtyard, painted in zebra stripes, was shaded by a huge tree, possibly a chestnut, and would have provided a pleasant place for gatherings, large and small (Figure 43). Slave owners certainly complained about one effect of slave gatherings – noise. Pliny the Younger, for example, was thankful for a room of his own that closed off the voices of his young slaves and, especially during the Saturnalia, segregated him from the celebrations of his household (*Letters* 2.27.20–24).

43. Peristyle in the service area of the Villa at Oplontis. The zebra stripes on the walls appear throughout the service area of the villa where the domestic slaves would have spend much of their time. This decoration distinguishes these rooms from the lavish paintings in the rest of the villa.

That slaves had families and social relations is clear not only from the master's law and literature, but from epitaphs written by and to slaves. Although relatively mute compared to Roman law and literature, these epitaphs testify to slaves' own perspective and the importance that they attached to these relations. Significantly, slaves writing in Latin used all the freeborn terms for family relations – wife/husband, father, mother, sister, brother – despite the legal and social denial of the legitimacy of slaves' family ties. Parents wrote epitaphs for children (and vice versa), like Aprodisia's dedication to her sixteen-year-old son, a slave and foot servant (Figure 44c); siblings commemorated each other, as in the epitaph of Sophro, the slave and accountant of Sisenna Statilius Taurus, consul in 16 CE, made by his sister Psyche and his wife Optata (Figure 44d). Most common are dedications by spouses,

(a)

(b)

(c)

(d)

44a–d. Epitaphs from the *columbarium* of the Statilii Tauri, Rome. (su concessione del Minstero per i Beni e le Attività Culturali – Soprintendenza Speciale per i Beni Archeologici di Roma) (a) Iucundus, slave of Taurus, litter bearer. As long as he lived, he was a man and acted on behalf of himself and others. As long as he lived, he lived honorably. Callista and Philologus dedicated (this). (*Corpus of Latin Inscriptions* 6.6308) (b) To Agatho, litter bearer. Caliste [*sic*], (his) vicaria, and Philologus and Felix (made this). (*Corpus of Latin Inscriptions* 6.6303) (c) Logas, slave of Messalina, foot servant, lived 16 years. Aprodisia [*sic*], (his) mother, made (this). (*Corpus of Latin Inscriptions* 6.6335) (d) Sophro, slave of Sisenna Statilius, accountant/ bookkeeper. Psyche, (his) sister, and Optata, (his) wife, made (this). (*Corpus of Latin Inscriptions* 6.6358) like the epitaphs written by the slaves Syntomus and Hellanicus to their respective wives, Galatea, a foot servant who died at age thirty-one, and Elate, a hairdresser in the household of the noble Volusii, dead at age twenty:

> Galatea, foot servant, lived 31 years.
> Syntomus husband.
> (Corpus of Latin Inscriptions 6.9776, Rome)

> To the Departed Spirits.
> Elate, hairdresser of Cornelia Volusia,
> lived twenty years. Hellanicus (made this)
> for a well-deserving wife.
> (Corpus of Latin Inscriptions 6.7296, Rome)

Although epitaphs cannot give us sociological certainty, scholars have used them to tease out the probable family patterns at least for urban slaves. Generally, slaves married slaves or freed slaves within the same household, as in the cases of Elate and Hellanicus and Sophro and Optata. Where one spouse was a slave at death, and the other a freedman or freedwoman, we catch one stage of a family history: in these cases, the marriage usually began with both partners in slavery; one partner was freed, while the other was still enslaved – perhaps later to achieve freedom. Any children born before the mother's manumission, however, remained slaves, whatever the status of the parents. Some wives were the *vicariae* (slaves of slaves) of their husbands: this may have been the case for Agatho, a litter bearer of the noble Statilii, and Callista (Caliste) (Figure 44b). Although Callista identifies herself as the slave of the slave Agatho, other epitaphs indicate that the *vicaria,* technically part of the slave's *peculium,* was often a wife. The epitaphs of Logas, Sophro, and Agatho also suggest another aspect of family. All of the epitaphs come from the same *columbarium,* and, in fact, Callista and Philologus also dedicated the epitaph of Iucundus, the litter bearer discussed at the beginning of the chapter. The family relations reflected in these epitaphs existed amid the larger life of the *familia,* the slaves and freedmen of a single owner's family.

The *familia* as a group was formally expressed in cult and, often, in an organization called a *collegium* (guild, club, society). Every Roman house had at least one shrine called a *lararium* dedicated to the deities that protected the house, household, and owner. Scholars believe that the shrines found in kitchens and work areas of the house were a focus for religious worship by the *familia* and were administered by its slaves and freedmen (see also Figure 6). The *lararium* in the House of Sutoria Primigenia at Pompeii includes perhaps a depiction of the *familia* at a ritual (Figure 45). Two oversized *lares* stand on each side of the scene. Toward the left near a flute player and over an altar are the Genius and Juno of the house (the guardian spirits of the head of the household, the *paterfamilias,* and his wife) or the *paterfamilias* and his wife – she in a *stola* and he in a toga pulled over his head to perform a sacrifice. To the right are two rows of thirteen individuals, slaves and freedmen, who are all dressed in white, short-sleeved tunics and who make the same gesture – their right hands at their waist and their left held to their chests. The large number of people in the scene is unusual for *lararia,* and we cannot be sure exactly what ritual is performed. However, the painting mirrors the formal constitution of the household with master and mistress at its head, gathered together at sacrifice: the relative size of the participants expresses the hierarchy within the household.

Collegia of various types were common in Roman society: there were burial *collegia* whose members shared the goal of named commemoration and occupational *collegia* whose members shared a trade. Inside the household, a domestic *collegium* joined slaves and freedmen of the same owner(s), who either supported such an organization of his slaves or at least allowed it to exist, perhaps as a gesture of kindness or for more instrumental reasons – binding slaves and freed slaves more firmly to his household. These *collegia,* then, represent a formal and sanctioned gathering of the slaves and freedmen of the family. Domestic *collegia* administered the tomb of the Volusii in which Elate was buried and the tomb of the Statilii in which Logas, Sophro, Agatho, and

45. *Lararium* painting in the House of Sutoria Primigenia (I.13.4), Pompeii. (Photo Michael Larvey su concessione del Minstero per i Beni e le Attività Culturali – Soprintendenza Speciale per i Beni Archeologici di Napoli e Pompei)

Iucundus were buried. Members of the *collegium* commemorated their fellow slaves and freed slaves, joined their fellows at special meals, and elected each other to an array of offices of the *collegium*.

Less official, and out of sight of the slaveholder or beneath his understanding, were the relations of slaves who belonged to the same household. The epitaphs of slaves testify to host of different relationships. In the tomb set aside for the freedmen and slaves of the Statilii, for example, Diomedes, slave and courier, is commemorated by his fellow slaves or housemates (*contubernales;* Figure 46a); Optata, slave and doorkeeper, by her friends (Figure 46b); and Messia, slave and spinner, by Iacinthus, slave and masseur:

> Messia, Dardanian, spinner.
> Iacinthus, masseur, Dardanian, made (this).
>
> (*Corpus of Latin Inscriptions* 6.6343, Rome)

We might suspect that Messia and Iacinthus were a couple, but the only stated relation between them is their shared origin: they both came from the same place in Asia Minor or from the same Illyrian tribe. Many slaves and freed slaves, regardless of their familial relations, identified themselves as fellow slaves (*conservi*) or fellow freed slaves (*colliberti*): even where we suspect marriage, they claimed their shared *familia*. Such epitaphs, then, reveal a community with multiple and complex relationships in which the relations of family overlap with those of *familia* – that is, shared slavery.

In his second century CE novel the *Metamorphoses,* Apuleius tells a story that, although it is a fiction, speaks of the reality of these kinds of overlapping relations, putting flesh on the bones of the epitaphs, so to speak (10.13–14). The narrator, who has been turned into an ass by magic, is sold to two brothers and fellow slaves who serve the same wealthy master: one is a pastry chef and the other a cook. They share a life and quarters. The ass narrator claims that he is welcomed as a third *contubernalis* (the word for a tent mate, a housemate, a close friend, or a slave's spouse). Each night, after their owner's luxurious

46a–b. Epitaphs from the *columbarium* of the Statilii Tauri, Rome. (su concessione del Minstero per i Beni e le Attività Culturali – Soprintendenza Speciale per i Beni Archeologici di Roma)

(a) To Diomedes, courier. (His) "housemates" give (this). (*Corpus of Latin Inscriptions* 6.6357)

(b) Optata, slave of Pansa [a freedman in the household], doorkeeper. (Her) friends made (this). (*Corpus of Latin Inscriptions* 6.6326)

dinner, the brothers and fellow slaves bring back to their quarters the lavish leftovers – the cook various meats and fish dishes and the pastry chef all sorts of sweet treats. Then they go off to the baths and return to banquet together. The ass, however, threatens to disrupt their companionship and mutual trust. He gobbles up the dishes when the brothers are at the baths, and each brother suspects the other. When they finally confront each other, a fight threatens to divide them, not as brothers but as partners, as one of the brothers remarks. They both take an oath that they have not stolen the food, and, relieved, they set about to discover the real culprit. The pair, fellow slaves and brothers, share quarters, a life, work, and the means of enjoying the "fruits" of their own labor; Apuleius's tale suggests, too, that the breakdown in trust disturbs them both.

In a different setting, the small shop, we find groups of fellow freedmen manumitted by the same individual or a couple. Like the two freedmen who met on the slave platform, these ex-slaves began their association in slavery, continued it into freedom, and commemorated it at death:

> For Publius Avillius Menander, the freedman of Publius, patron, after his death his freedmen made (this) and for themselves who are named below:
> Avillia Philusa (deceased), the freedwoman of Publius;
> Publius Avillius Hilarus, the freedman of Publius;
> Publius Avillius Anteros, the freedman of Publius;
> Publius Avillius Felix, the freedman of Publius;
> Tailors on the smaller Cermalus.
> (*Corpus of Latin Inscriptions* 6.33920, Rome)

Philusa, dead at the time of the writing of the epitaph, Hilarus, Anteros, and Felix, all tailors in a shop on the Cermalus, the western slope of the Palatine Hill in Rome, provided a tomb for themselves and their ex-master, Menander, a freedman himself, whose occupation they did not name. As slaves and then as free men and woman, they worked together in the same shop. Whether they were related, or two of them married, or they made other bonds among themselves, they acted like a family, taking over the family's traditional responsibility to bury its dead – for themselves, their patron, and their fellow freedmen. If the epitaph mirrors the lives of these people, shared work and shared slavery linked these men and woman, and the absence of their patron's occupational title highlights their own bond as fellow tailors and freedmen.

Whether as substitute or supplement, the relations of *familia* perhaps compensated for the loss of family and for the limits on family life effected by slavery. Beyond disease and death that threatened every Roman family, slaves faced additional difficulties forming and maintaining families. The ratio of male to female slaves in individual households had repercussions for both enslaved men and women. In three of the large tombs devoted to the slaves and ex-slaves of wealthy families in Rome, male slaves outnumbered female slaves. Historians have suggested that this sexual imbalance reflects the actual composition of urban households. If this figure approximates ancient reality, then male slaves may have had trouble finding a partner. Many would have had to go outside the household to do so. In these cases, although the slave spouses lived in the same city, they served and lived in different locations. If other households had a similar imbalance of the sexes, some enslaved men had no opportunities for marriage. Enslaved men, along with poor free men, were the major clientele of the many prostitutes in the city, so female prostitution provided temporary sexual relations, at least, for partnerless male slaves.

For female slaves, the sexual imbalance in the urban household meant a choice of partners or pressure to choose. If, however, the sexual imbalance in three large tombs in Rome indicates that wealthy slaveholders sought to limit the numbers of female slaves in their households, then some enslaved women – most probably girls – faced grim alternatives, suggests historian Susan Treggiari:

> Some girls are kept to work in the city household, others might perhaps be kept for their parents' sake and as the *delicia* (favorites or pets) of their owners, others might disappear to country estates to work wool and produce children. ... The prospects for girls who were sold would, if most rich families had a surplus of girls, be gloomy, the most likely purchasers

being brothel-keepers or poor people who wanted a drudge. (1975a: 400–401)

If slavery limited the marital opportunities of slave men, it also used slave women to fill the gap through prostitution, and slaveholders profited on both sides – from the price received for girls sold and from the fees charged for prostitutes' sexual labor.

There is less information on slave family relations in the country. Agricultural writers mention few female jobs, but this may just reflect the major concerns of these writers – agriculture, viticulture, and husbandry – to which the female tasks of food preparation, spinning, and clothes making were secondary. As mentioned above, these writers mention slave wives only as rewards for the good work of slave managers, foremen, herdsmen, and shepherds or as a technique of control to keep enslaved men at their work; the manuals mention the children of these couples only as additions to the estate and its slave staff. Some historians argue that the presence of women and children on Italy's farms and estates in fact meant family life for slaves in the countryside. Certainly, the enslaved men, women, and children in these relations did not view them from their owners' instrumental perspective; for them, at least, their connections to slave spouses and children were family relations, not spurs to labor or means of control. However, what exactly "family relations" meant and, for that matter, what they were like are questions that are difficult to answer.

Living conditions and work, too, must have shaped family life. Marital and family relations took place in proximity to other slaves in the household in shared living areas or work space – and, of course, to the slaves' owners. The literary, legal, and material sources for slave housing make it doubtful that every couple – much less the couple and their children – had even their own small room. In large houses, like Pliny's, there was a *paedagogium,* an establishment for training young slaves, which included quarters for the boys (*Letters* 7.27.13). The evidence raises questions about the lived realities of family life for the slaves discussed above. What did this mean for time spent with parents?

When were boys separated from parents? How soon did Logas, for example, begin his work as a foot servant? How often did his mother see him? If Galatea, the foot servant, slept on her owner's doorstep or at the foot of her bed, as we know some personal servants did, when and how did she spend time with her husband Syntomus? If Elate, the hairdresser, was at the command of her mistress, how did this affect her relationship with Hellanicus, her husband?

Ultimately, slave families were vulnerable because they existed at the will of the master. Sale, always a possibility, split children and parents, husbands and wives, and siblings. The death of the slave owner, too, could mean the division of a family when the owner left slave family members to different heirs. The marriage of a slave owner's daughter could mean the separation of those slaves who formed part of her dowry. Equally, loans, mortgages, and gifts might divide parents and children or siblings.

Slaveholders' sexual relations with their own slaves, male as well as female, too, could disrupt slaves' families and love affairs. Roman authors frequently mention the master's "boy," a slave who was the object of his owner's desire. Sexual relations with enslaved women are assumed, and although a master might be criticized for his lack of self-control, a man's sexual relations with his slave women were not seen as shameful, much less wrong (women's sexual relations with their male slaves, however, were subject to vehement objections). In the first century CE, the biographer and moralist Plutarch recommends that a man whose sexual pleasures are excessive and dissolute should show respect for his wife by visiting such pleasures on female slaves (*Moralia* 140B). Children born from such unions were the subjects of jokes about their owners, and they show up as a concern in the law on property. In other words, the physical vulnerability of slaves expressed itself not only in corporal punishment but also in their sexual availability. Law patrolled men's sexual treatment of other owners' slaves but put few limits on an owner's relations with his own slaves. Slaves had little control in situations where the owner or his son took a sexual hankering for a daughter, son, wife, or loved one. In one case, the master's interference may have resulted in a violent assault: according to Tacitus, the murder of Pedanius Secundus might have been provoked by Secundus's interference with the sexual partner of the slave who killed him (*Annals* 14.42.1).

Sale, the death of the master, his legal right to loan, gift, or mortgage his slaves, and his ability to assert his will sexually or otherwise all belong to what the historian David Brion Davis calls the "radical uncertainty and unpredictability [that] was characteristic of all slave systems" (2001: 126). Regardless of the lived differences among slaves – gender, occupation, privileges, personality, and the character of their owners – the very institution of slavery brought uncertainty into the life of all slaves, both litter bearers like Iucundus and imperial bureaucrats like Musicus Scurranus. The essential definition of the slave as property at the disposal of the slave owner and the owner's power over the slave trumped all the slave's human relations – family, friends, and fellow slaves as well as cordial relations with a kind and benevolent slaveholder. The slaveholder's death, the events in his or her family, and economic decisions could and did translate into the slave's separation from parents, children, siblings, friends, and community. Slave owners' power over the bodies of their slaves meant that no slave, regardless of occupation, gender, or favored relations with the slaveholder, was safe from arbitrary physical violence and sexual assault. Even Seneca, who urges self-control in the punishment of slaves and himself prefers verbal correction, never denies the slave owner's physical power. In his philosophical tract on anger, he remarks that waiting, instead of acting immediately on an impulse to flog a slave or break his legs, does not erase masterly power: "Such power (*potestas*) will not perish, if it is deferred" (*On Anger* 3.32.2). The whims of slaveholders, their wills, their moods, and their desires, determined the physical safety and integrity of their slaves.

How did slaves live with radical uncertainty, with the violence that surrounded them, and, more generally, with the practices of mastery that controlled their lives and attempted to extract the most labor possible from them? Generally, historians have seen slaves' response in terms of the opposition between accommodation and resistance: accommodation refers to slaves' acceptance of their servitude and their attempts to live the life of the slaveholder's "good slave"; resistance refers to slaves' rejection of their servitude and actions that oppose their condition and their owner's will. Messenio, the good slave from Plautus's *Menaechmi,* and Spartacus model the extremes of accommodation and resistance. Messenio, the "good slave," is at pains to obey his master's every wish and, fearing punishment, puts his master before all else. Spartacus, the "rebel slave," not only escaped with his fellow slaves and gladiators but also led a massive slave revolt that took several Roman armies three years to squelch.

In fact, between the rare massive slave revolt and the submissive behavior of a Messenio, there was a wide range of behaviors reported by slaveholders. Their views, discussed at the beginning of this chapter and reconsidered in a different light here, suggest the actions taken by slaves themselves. Some slaves, as in the cases of Pedanius Secundus and Larcius Macedo, attacked and even killed their masters when the latter welched on an agreed price for manumission, interfered in slaves' love lives, or acted cruelly. Law tried to ensure that slaves acted to protect owners: when a slaveholder was murdered, all of his or her slaves, guilty or innocent, could be tortured and executed if they resided in the same house as their owner. The jurist Ulpian observes: "no home can be safe except if slaves are compelled to guard their masters both from members of the household and from outsiders at the risk of their own lives" (*Digest* 29.5.1). Some slaves evidently removed themselves from an owner's power by killing themselves: the law mentions slaves who throw themselves into the Tiber, off a bridge, or from a height and those who take poison or strangle themselves (*Digest* 21.1.17.4 and 6, 21.1.23.3).

Less violent, although no less emphatic about their refusal of their condition, were slaves who fled their masters: as Roman jurists acknowledged, "flight is a form of liberty in that the slave is for the present relieved of his master's power" (*Digest* 21.1.17.10). Judging by the extensive discussion and regulations in Roman law, the flight of slaves obsessed slaveholders and, we must suppose, was an action taken by many slaves, despite the many difficulties faced by the fugitive – slave catchers, the surveillance of local and provincial officials, and the penalties for those who harbored runaway slaves. There was no free North to which Roman slaves might escape, as there was for slave fugitives in the nineteenth-century United States. The problem for the Roman slave fugitives was where to hide or how to disguise themselves as free people. What slaves knew of the world outside their households or farms helped or hindered them. For some, especially enslaved women with children, the bonds of family tethered them to their place.

Slaves left their owner's control temporarily without the intention of fleeing permanently. Some evidently hid out from an angry owner and returned once his temper cooled down (*Digest* 21.1.17.4). Others went to visit a relative or to return to a mother (*Digest* 21.1.17.5). Still others were simply truants: in the words of a Roman jurist, the *erro* (truant or wanderer) "indulges in aimless roaming and, after wasting time on trivialities, returns home at a late hour" *(Digest* 21.1.17.14). City slaves, complains Columella, spend their time idling, gambling, or visiting the public square, the circus, the theaters, the taverns, or the brothels (1.8.2).

Above all, Roman lawyers and writers complain about theft by slaves – in the household, on farms, on ships, in workshops, in the army camp, and even at the undertaker's, where a slave robs the corpses he is supposed to prepare for burial. What slaves could appropriate of their owner's property – or steal from them, in slaveholders' point of view – depended in large measure on their occupations. Columella complains of rural slaves stealing grain from the threshing room floor (1.7.6). A literate steward or accounts keeper could fix the books and get away with substantial property. The runaway house servant might risk taking money, silver, or costly items. Some slaves stole other slaves: often, that is, they ran away with their *vicariae,* who in many cases would have been spouses. For the most part, slave thefts were what the law called "domestic thefts" (*domestica furta*) – petty and not worth public action (*Digest* 48.19.11.1). Pliny the Elder complains that in contrast to the good old days when slaves belonged to the master's family, today's slaves, a crowd of foreigners, steal so regularly that food and wine need to be locked up (*Natural History* 33.26).

Other activities that troubled slaveholders, and point to slave responses to their condition, did damage to property and interfered with work. Slaves, willfully and by accident, burnt down villas, farmhouses, and tenement buildings. Others, at least by their owners' account, did their work poorly; we might wonder about a variety of causes – illness, mood, resistance, or an assertion over the timing and rhythm of their own labor. According to Columella, slaves out of the slaveholder's control or without the strong hand of a capable *vilicus* let oxen out for hire, do not feed animals properly, fail to plow carefully, claim to sow more than they actually have, and thresh grain wastefully or steal it. They do not prevent the thefts of other slaves and do not honestly record how much grain is stored. Given the opportunity, slaves are lazy, loitering, time wasting, and they sleep away the day – city slaves most of all, who spend their time daydreaming about the pleasures of the city, as noted above. Some slaves feign illness; others are insolent and often must be chained (1.7.6, 1.8.2). From the point of view of resistance, the mental defects listed in the Edict of the Aediles – obstinacy, impudence, recklessness, hot temper, quarreling – all name behavior that troubled slaveholders and indicate a lack of easy accommodation to servitude.

All of these reports of slave behavior come only from sources written by and for slaveholders, and upper-class slaveholders at that. The view of our sources poses several problems of interpretation. For one, did slave owners report what slaves actually did? As discussed above, slaveholding Romans had a stereotype of the slave as greedy, untrustworthy, and lazy. That stereotype may have functioned as a lens through which they observed slaves' actions. Slaveholders, too, judged the acts of slaves as evidence of mental or moral flaws or failures. In Roman law, for example, runaways, truants, and obstinate or insolent slaves all have a mental defect. Columella's diatribe on lazy, daydreaming city slaves, his complaints about the negligence and greed of rural slaves, and Pliny the Elder's rant about hordes of pilfering slaves all speak in moralistic terms. When Tacitus and Pliny report the murder of Pedanius Secundus and Larcius Macedo, they dismiss the motives of the slave murderers and see the acts as criminal and unreasonable.

Despite the negative point of view, several factors suggest that the behavior, if not its interpretation, reflects the actual daily interactions of Roman slave owners and slaves. First, not only do law and literature repeat similar instances, but the provision of legal recourses suggests that, in fact, slave owners experienced a need to patrol slave behavior. Second, both slaveholders and slaves from other slave societies report similar behavior – flight, truancy, theft, feigning illness, failure to work at the master's pace. The question, then, is to separate behavior and interpretation. The stereotypes of slaves and slaveholders' complaints represent slave owners' interpretation of slave behavior, and we are not bound to accept that understanding and explanation. It is important to see that the very naming of slave behavior stacks the deck. Terms like insolence or impudence put a particular spin on the action of a slave who sought to explain his behavior, who disagreed with his master, or who refused to accept criticism without a response. When Columella accuses slaves of stealing grain, he criminalizes slaves' appropriation of what their labor produced – or, in some cases, food for survival. In another view, the "truant" slave took time for himself or took his time doing his assigned tasks.

There is no direct testimony from Roman slaves, but American slave narratives show us that slaves could see their behavior in different terms than their owners and could pierce their owners' moral presumptions. The famous autobiography of Frederick Douglass is especially useful for thinking about Roman slaves. First, his account reflects observations made in many other slave narratives on the subject of insolence and theft. Second, since Douglass often comments on the nature of slavery itself and especially the relations between master and slave, his account at times seems like a theory of slavery.

At one point in his story, his owner has sent him to a slave breaker, an individual whose treatment subdued recalcitrant slaves. Brutalized by the cruelty of the breaker, Douglass fled to his owner to report on his treatment. His owner

> had no doubt I deserved the flogging. He did not believe I was sick – I was only endeavoring to get rid of work. My dizziness was laziness, and [the breaker] did right to flog me as he had done. ... I must not assert my innocence of the allegations he had piled up against me, for that would be impudence. The guilt of a slave was always and everywhere presumed. ... The word of the slave against this presumption was generally treated as impudence, worthy of punishment. "Do you dare to contradict me, you rascal?" was the final silencer of counter statements from the lips of a slave. (1962 [1892]: 132)

In Douglass's view, not only were the relations of master and slave shaped by the slaveholder's belief in the slave's dishonesty, they were characterized by a process of renaming – the slave's illness becomes laziness, his assertions of innocence impudence. Ultimately, the slave owner's concern for his own power ("do you dare to contradict me") demanded that his terms for the slave's behavior stood as the truth. And punishment – or its threat – silenced the slave's assertions.

Douglass's account of his first thefts from this owner highlights the slave's process of naming in which his explanation of stealing reconfigures the meaning of property. He and his fellow slaves were "so wretchedly starved ... that we were compelled to live at the expense of our neighbors, or to steal from the home larder" (104). Struggling with the morality of his actions, Douglass comes to a different moral and economic logic, one that was "not much known or respected" by masters (63):

> After much reflection I reasoned myself into the conviction that there was no other way to do, and that after all there was no wrong in it. Considering that my labor and person were the property of Master Thomas and that I was deprived of the

necessaries of life – necessaries obtained by my own labor – it was easy to deduce the right to supply myself with what was my own. It was simply appropriating what was my own to the use of my master, since the health and strength derived from such food were exerted in his service. (104–105)

Beyond the occasional assertion on a tombstone like that made by Iucundus, litter bearer, Roman slaves have not left such eloquent observations about their actions, but we can expect that, like Douglass, they will have attached other meanings to their acts than those of their owners. Historians of slavery, ancient and modern, have argued about the meaning of such slave behaviors. Some interpret them as individual acts of frustration or expressions of anger that provide temporary relief but do not threaten the slave system; others see them as a form of troubling the master. Following the kind of sentiments expressed by Douglass and other former slaves, historians of American slavery understand such actions as the ways slaves asserted some control over their labor, claimed time for themselves, and appropriated what was needed or wanted for body and soul. The historian of American slavery Stephanie Camp reminds us that however *we* interpret slaves' behavior, "slave resistance was a fact of life … constituted … in the slavery experience itself" (2004: 2). Its daily, ordinary quality makes it a part of the everyday relations of slave owners and slaves – in other words, part of the slave system itself. Where Pliny talks in terms of state and citizenship, Columella perhaps comes closer to the lived world of his slaves, when he talks about the daily, continuous need to watch and control slaves' tasks, time, and what for him are their petty but vexing failures to enact their owner's will.

The individual and particular experiences and lives of Roman slaves would have mixed accommodation and resistance rather than set them at odds. Different slaves would have engaged each differently. Yet as the Roman historian Brent Shaw observes, the relations between those individual slaves and the institution of slavery "can only be measured by the constraints necessary to keep them 'in place'";

where slaves seem to have consented to their condition or accommodated themselves to it, that accommodation was "achieved by systemic compulsion" (1998: 49). The Roman fabulist Phaedrus, a slave freed by the emperor Augustus, claims that compulsion in fact often silenced the open assertions of slaves:

> Now, I will briefly show why this genre of stories was invented. Since the slave who is vulnerable to punishment did not dare to say what he wanted to, he transferred his real feelings into fables, and through funny stories tricked his way out of a reputation for trouble making. (3.prologue.33–37)

What slaves had to say was redirected into covert modes of expression or genres, like fables, which were also a form used by slaves in the nineteenth-century American South. Such forms allowed slaves to elude their owners' charges of insolence or disloyalty and a whipping or a slap that might be the reward of straightforward talk.

Fables are notoriously difficult to interpret, but Phaedrus's fable of the wolf and the dog (3.7) speaks eloquently of the limits of even a comfortable slavery, the so-called favors of paternalistic masters, and the pleasure of freedom. In Phaedrus's fable, a hungry, skinny wolf encounters a well-fed dog and wants to know why he looks so sleek. The dog explains that he is the guardian of his master's house and protects it from thieves at night. He receives bread without asking; his master gives him bones from his own table; the slave servants offer him scraps and leftovers. Without any effort on his part, his belly is filled up. The wolf is ready to sign up for service, when he notices that a chain has worn down the dog's neck. When the wolf asks the dog about his condition, the dog replies that it's really nothing: because his masters think that he is excitable, they tie him up during the day. But at night he is untied and goes wherever he likes. The wolf wants to know if the dog can leave if he likes, and, of course, the answer is no. "Enjoy what you praise," says the wolf, "I don't want to play the part of a king, if I am not free." The dog's kindly master may feed him well, but the master's perception of the dog keeps him on a chain during the day and prohibits him from leaving at night. No matter how well fed, the dog or the slave is bound. "How sweet is freedom, I will briefly reveal," announces Phaedrus in the opening of his fable: better hunger, rain, snow, and a hard life in the woods than a full belly, if it means chains and no freedom to go where you like.

CHAPTER 5

SLAVES AT WORK:
IN THE FIELDS, THE
HOUSEHOLD, AND THE
MARKETPLACE

Where urban slaves have been bequeathed, some authorities distinguish them not by their place but by their work, so that even if they are on country estates but do not do country work they are held to be urban slaves. But it should be said that urban slaves must be understood to be those whom the head of the household used to count as his urban slaves, which is best gathered from the list of his staff and also from his ration allowances. (*Digest* 32.1.99pr., trans. A. Watson)

This lazy and sleepy kind of slaves, used to leisure, the public square, the circus, and the theaters, to gambling, taverns, brothels, always dreams about these follies. (Columella, *On Agriculture* 1.8.2)

Messia, Dardanian, spinner.
Iacinthus, masseur, Dardanian, made (this).
(*Corpus of Latin Inscriptions* 6.6343, Rome)

R oman slave owners divided slaves into two categories: city slaves and country slaves, the *familia urbana* and the *familia rustica*. However, in the opinion of Roman jurists, the slave's actual work was more fundamental than where he or she did it: certain jobs were typically urban; others involved various kinds of farming. Thus, owners' own lists of their slaves and their rations had to enter any calculation of category. Columella, too, distinguished slaves by place and work, but for him the city was a place for idle slaves who filled their days with the stereotypical vices of slaves – drinking, gambling, eating, and sex. They entertained themselves at the theater, games, and races, and frequented the lowliest, most vulgar sites – bars and brothels.

Messia, the slave spinning woman, and Iacinthus, the slave masseur, belonged to the staff that served the noble Statilii Tauri in the city of Rome. Messia's epitaph tells us little about them beyond their jobs and their origin, Phrygia or perhaps Illyria (see Chapter 4). For Columella, they belonged to that sluggish kind of slaves with little to do and lots of time for fun and games. We might wonder, however, why Iacinthus commemorated his fellow countrywoman and himself by their occupations, if work was not vital to their sense of themselves. Modern historians see different messages in Iacinthus's and Messia's job titles: their pride in their work, their place in the household, an assertion of a physical efficacy, or, perhaps, even a short-hand biography.

Albeit in different ways and from different points of view, slaves and slaveholders found the slave's work significant. This is not surprising, for, above all, slavery is and was a form of dependent labor – a system where some control and benefit from the labor of others. This chapter explores the labor of enslaved men, women, and children. The facts of slave labor may, at first glance, seem rather dry. Yet when we move beyond a recital of specific jobs, workplaces, and laboring conditions, the study of slaves' work is especially illuminating for an understanding of both Roman society and Roman slaves. Slaves were nearly everywhere – in the fields, houses, workshops, and markets of the Roman world. Slaves at work shaped the Roman economy and social order, and the labor assigned by slaveholders shaped the slaves themselves and their experience of slavery. For slave men and women, work was what they did all day. It affected their health, movement, family lives, living conditions, and access to resources and recreations (although not quite in the way Columella imagined). Work informed relations with their owners, fellow slaves, and individuals outside of the households to which they belonged. For some, work provided avenues for accumulation and even freedom. Throughout the discussion of various types of slave labor that follows, it is useful to keep in mind the tensions between slaveholders whose power assigned the slaves' work and the slaves whose agency performed it in their own particular ways.

Work as Institution and Experience

The passages quoted above suggest how the question of work addresses a particularly close intersection of slavery as an institution and slavery as the experience of individuals. Three aspects of the institution are of concern here: slaves' roles in the economy, their place in Roman society, and the effects of slavery on Roman values and attitudes. If we focus on the Roman economy and look at the varied evidence of slave labor, we find slaves in nearly every type of work except soldiering. Beyond their particular jobs, slave men and women occupied certain key roles in the Roman economy. On country estates, they produced the income of the upper classes. Slaves also served in the domestic households of the wealthy and, like other possessions, displayed the class and social standing of their owners. Both as farm labor and as domestic servants, slaves held a critical place in Roman society for ordinary Roman citizens as well as the elite. Keith Hopkins sets out the way slave labor shaped social relations in the Roman Republic during the wars of conquest in the third and second centuries BCE:

> Thus one of the main functions of slavery was that it allowed the elite to increase the discrepancy between rich and poor without alienating the free citizen peasantry from their willingness to fight in wars for the further expansion of empire; slavery also allowed the rich to recruit labour to work their estates in a society which had no labour market; and it permitted ostentatious display, again without the direct exploitation of the free poor. Slavery made it unnecessary for the rich to employ the poor directly, except as soldiers. (1978: 14)

In addition, slaves acted as managers and business agents for the rich, and complex legal stipulations enabled slaves to engage in commerce on behalf of elite owners, keeping the elite at a distance from the marketplace, which, as explained below, the upper classes considered vulgar. Further down the social scale, slaves worked for ordinary Romans, some of them ex-slaves themselves. They served food and drink in taverns, mucked about in the tubs of ancient laundries, labored in bakeries, and produced a variety of goods in urban workshops.

Slavery shaped the attitudes of the freeborn toward work and money making. Except for a romantic view of the ancient farmer-soldier, Latin literature does not celebrate work, money making, or financial success in the marketplace. Roman authors express the elite's disdain for work, worker, and small-scale commerce. In a variety of texts, stereotypes depict servants as obnoxious, doctors and teachers as dangerous, and businessmen as liars. Waiters ignore poor freeborn Romans at the dinner table of the servants' wealthy owner, and his doorkeeper snubs them. Teachers corrupt their students, and doctors kill their patients. Businessmen cheat their customers, and they are crass and materialistic. For Cicero, all craftsmen practice a lowly trade. And anyone whose activities serve physical pleasure deserves no respect: this includes retailers of food, cooks, perfume dealers, dancers, and the performers of low-class song and dance acts (*On Duties* 1.150).

In the imagination of Roman authors, the very nature of these occupations dishonors their practitioners. Their activities are dirty, their skills base. Servants may insult the poor man, but they themselves must please their owners: for Seneca, waiters, carvers, cooks, and provisioners all do the same worthless thing – satisfying their owners' physical appetites and demands (*Moral Letters* 47.2–8). Tradesmen may achieve financial success, but their work is sordid or vulgar. In the view of Roman authors, those who succeed in the marketplace are always skilled at flattery, which, for the freeborn, is simply a form of pleasing: such men willingly do what others want them to do and mold their behavior to the desires of others. For the freeborn author, such behavior evokes the image of the slave, who has no choice but to please.

Occupation, then, could always be used to dishonor wealthy merchants and dismiss any claim to social standing. Money allows them to buy a privileged seat in the theater, equestrian status, or the honor of giving games, but since they were originally auctioneers, barbers, or shoemakers, they remain lowly, despite the signs of purchased rank.

The wage laborer (*mercennarius*) ranked as the lowliest because his condition approached that of the slave. Not only did he do manual labor, he also worked for another. He hired out his labor to another person rather than entering into a contract to produce an object or service. By selling his labor, the *mercennarius* sold himself, for, regardless of legal distinctions, the laborer was not separated from his labor. Hiring out his labor potentially reduced him to the state of something owned – an animal, inanimate object, a slave. That is why Cicero comments that the wages of *mercennarii* were the reward of slavery, and some hundred years later, Seneca could call the slave a perpetual *mercennarius* (*On Benefits* 3.22.1).

When we look into the discrete lives of thousands of individual slaves, their owners, and Romans who were not slaveholders but lived in a slave society, we ask about experience and about how individuals lived the institution of slavery. It is, of course, impossible to account for the working lives of all Roman slaves; however, we can look at three important sites of work and the occupations of slaves in them. The rest of the chapter examines slave labor in the countryside, in the large households of the elite, and in the shops and workshops of the city. In each section, after a survey of slave occupations, the discussion turns to the conditions of work and then to the ways slaves lived within those conditions and shaped them.

In the Fields

The work of rural slaves depended on the type and size of the farms on which they labored, and here the focus is on the western empire, especially Italy. Some landholders cultivated a single crop for production for the market – olives, grapes, or grain; others raised cattle or sheep; and still others grew fruits and vegetables for the local city market. Many, even those devoted to monoculture, also grew grain and raised animals. On small farms, whether owned by free peasants or rented by tenants, slave men and women lived and labored by their owners' sides at a variety of tasks without having one particular job. On larger farms and estates, the slaveholder's ideal was specialization, as Columella spells out for the mid-first century CE:

> The tasks of slaves should not be mixed up, so that all of them do the same thing. This is not advantageous to the farmer, either because none believes that his work is his own, or because, when he exerts himself, he performs a service that is not his but common to all, and so he evades his work. … For this reason, plowmen must be distinguished from vine workers, and vine workers from plowmen, and both of them from common laborers. (1.9.5–6)

Drawing on the jobs mentioned in Columella's agricultural manual, Figure 47 indicates the variety of labor performed by slaves. Enslaved and freed men involved in administration, record keeping, storage and distribution, and a few domestic positions (for example, *actor, atriensis, cellarius, procurator*) performed tasks that were also typical of urban slaves in the households of the elite. Certain supervisors worked only in the country (*magister operum, magister pecoris, magister singulorum officiorum, monitor,* and *vilicus;* see below). For the rest, agricultural labor included slaves who took care of particular animals – sheep and cattle, chickens, pigs, horses and mules, bees, and fish. Some labored in the fields – plowing, digging and cultivating, mowing, and reaping (Figure 48). Still others worked in olive groves and oil production, and perhaps most skilled were those who tended the vineyards and made wine (Figures 49–50). At times of the year when the work was heaviest, the harvest, for example, many, regardless of their assigned jobs, must have pitched in to help (for other depictions of agricultural workers, see Figure 36).

actor	• overseer, foreman
alligator	• vine binder
arator	• plowman
arborator	• tree pruner
atriensis	• majordomo or house cleaner and housekeeper
auceps	• bird catcher
aviarius	• poultry keeper
bublcus	• plowman
caprarius	• goat herder
capulator	• oil drawer
cellarius	• provisioner
curator	• keeper, guardian (of animals)
custos	• keeper (of animals), guardian, or overseer
custos vivarius	• gamekeeper
ergastularius	• jailer (in charge of the *ergastulum*)
faeni sector or *faenisex*	• hay cutter, mower
faber	• smith, craftsman, worker
fartor	• poultry fattener
fossor	• digger
holitor	• gardener
iugarius	• oxen keeper
magister operum	• foreman, overseer
magister pecoris	• head shepherd
magister singulorum officiorum	• foreman, overseer
mediastinus	• worker, common laborer
messor	• reaper
olearius	• oil maker, oil presser
operarius	• laborer
opilio	• shepherd
pampinator	• vine trimmer
pastinator	• cultivator, trench digger
pastor	• herdsman
pastor gallinarum	• poultry keeper
porculator	• pig breeder
procurator	• manager
promus	• provisioner
putator	• pruner
stabularius	• stable keeper
subulcus	• pig herder
veterinarius	• animal doctor
vilica	• wife of the *vilicus*, supervisor
vilcus	• manager of farm and slaves
vindemiator	• grape picker
vinitor	• vineyard worker, vine dresser

47. Jobs of rural slaves in Columella's *On Agriculture*. This list omits jobs that are described rather than titled, such as women who spin wool and also work in the field. (Adapted from K. R. Bradley, *Slavery and Society at Rome* [Cambridge: Cambridge University Press, 1994], p. 60, Table 2, with permission of Cambridge University Press)

48. Mosaic of plowing, digging, and sowing, Cherchell, third century CE.
(Courtesy Katherine M. D. Dunbabin)

49. Mosaics of vintage work, St-Romain-en-Gal, early third century CE. An agricultural calendar depicts workers gathering grapes, treading grapes, and cleaning up storage jars. (Réunion des Musées Nationaux/Art Resource, New York)

It is clear from off-hand references in the agricultural writers that children and women worked on the farm. Ideally, the *vilicus* (slave manager) began his training in boyhood, and other boys and girls were assigned a variety of tasks – cutting ferns, watching fowl, tending flocks, trimming vines, and food preparation. The chief female slave was the *vilica,* the wife of the slave manager, who had wide supervisory duties. The women awarded to shepherds and herdsmen tended to their needs and prepared their food. Cheese making, cooking, and spinning were specifically female jobs, and the historian Ulrike Roth has argued that slave women's production of cloth and rough clothing enriched their owners (2007). Some enslaved women worked in the fields and tended animals (keeping track of fowl was a task assigned to old women).

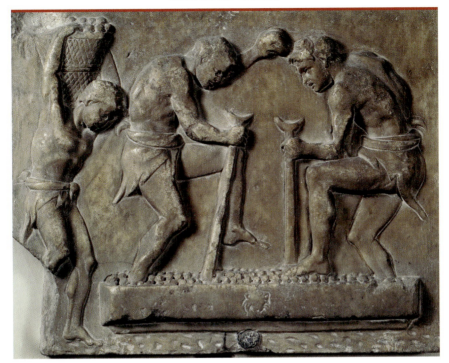

50. Relief of treading grapes, Venice, second century BCE. (Scala/Art Resource, New York)

Before turning to a specific example of slave labor in agriculture, we must consider a more general question that has occupied historians of slavery: How was this labor organized? Our evidence for Rome depends primarily on the manuals of Cato, Varro, and Columella, supplemented by passages from other sources. The three extant manuals span nearly 200 years, discuss different crops and animal husbandry, and mix different labor regimes. Moreover, different regions, crops, and slave demography affected the organization of labor. All three writers stress the need of close, careful supervision by the *vilicus,* the slave manager, and Varro and Columella talk about various kinds of foremen. Columella used gang labor: a group of slaves, directed by an overseer, worked the entire day in a routinized way. In Columella's view, this organization of labor facilitates close supervision and stimulates a competition that makes the punishment of laggards acceptable.

Yet at the same time, in all three manuals, we find evidence of the task system: the slaveholder assigned an activity for the day, and slaves set their own pace. The manuals include calculations of tasks by *iugera* and days: how many *iugera* of land can be plowed by so many workers in so many days; how many *iugera* of vines can be trimmed and dressed; how many *iugera* of meadows can be cut in a day. Some of these calculations account for slaves' pacing their own work: Saserna, an agricultural writer of the early first century BCE, calculated that one man could dig up a *iugerum* of land in four days, but he allowed thirteen days for the task to account for bad weather, illness, idleness, and negligence (Varro 1.16.5). The latter three factors typified slaveholders' complaints that bespeak both slaves' resistance and their attempt to assert some control over their labor (see below).

Apparently, gang and task labor were used in different places at different times and, on the same farm, for different sorts of labor. Vines required constant care and attention and were perhaps cultivated by small gangs. Planting and harvesting, which required many hands and involved intense labor for a defined period of time, too, was perhaps undertaken by gangs. Roman slaveholders' obsession with slave laziness, and the agricultural writers' concern to keep slaves busy, should make us wonder just how much free time slaves had, however their labor was organized.

Rural slaves have left no written accounts, and there are few epitaphs of these enslaved men and women. Historians must patch together bits and pieces from the archaeological remains of villas and farmsteads, law, and literature, especially the agricultural manuals, to describe the lives of these men and women and the conditions in which they lived and labored. Even where the agricultural writers set out ideals and even where they used farming for rhetorical purposes other than instructions in agriculture, they had to write in line with the vision and experience of their class, and all were themselves slaveholders who farmed for profit. Below, I translate Columella's own practices and his instructions to his readers into a picture of the working conditions of agricultural slaves in the first century CE – with a warning that Columella cannot account for every slave owner, even every wealthy owner who farmed his land with slave labor. For all rural slaves, however, it is useful to keep in mind the basic condition of slavery itself: the lives of all slaves depended on their individual slave owners' needs, decisions, and characters.

Columella focused on a farm that included olive groves, vineyards, land for grain, and pasturage for domestic animals. The owner lived in a comfortable residence, separated from the farmhouse (*villa rustica*) that housed the slaves along with facilities necessary for production – threshing floor, mill and bakery ovens, press rooms, stalls and pens (see Figure 41). For the slaves, although, of course, they went out to the fields, pastures, and vineyards, "home" was also a workplace where in bad weather or on short days they labored at other tasks (see below). Columella assumes that food was prepared and served to slaves in common; workers' clothing was made by slave women and distributed by the owner, slave manager, or his wife, who also passed out articles of everyday use.

Slaveholders' ideal of the full employment of slaves, in practice, meant long, full workdays. Slave workers left the farmstead at dawn and returned at twilight. Ideally, they were so tired after work that they thought only of food, rest, and sleep – and not what Columella saw as trouble making. The proper clothing ensured their ability to work in the cold and rain. A host of indoor tasks filled slave hours when days were short, the weather bad, or the sowing finished: sharpening tools, making poles and props for the vineyards, baskets, brooms, and hampers, and ties crafted out of willows. When rain, frost, or cold prohibited slave women from working in the fields, they were supposed to spin wool. Columella, like Varro 100 years earlier, advised landowners to have on hand twice the number of tools as slaves, so there would be not only no need to borrow from neighbors but also no need for slaves to take a break. Columella sets out a detailed calendar of activities that, if followed, left little time for anything but work. Toward the end of January, for example, after hoeing the wheat fields, Columella's slave laborers were not done: "those who have labor to spare" should hoe the barley fields and then move on to the bean fields (11.2.9–10). The Roman religious calendar was full of holidays, and we know from other sources that there were holidays specifically for slaves. However, while Columella mentions holidays on the farm in scattered places in his manual, work, not time off, is his preoccupation, and he has a long list of tasks that could be performed even on holidays.

In theory, all slaves from the ordinary laborer to the slave manager were subject to constant supervision. In the slaveholder's view, this kept them on schedule and busy, discouraged shirking and malingering, and avoided damage and carelessness. At the farmstead, the *vilica* watched for "lazy" field workers who had not gone out to the fields with the other slaves, and she sent the sick and tired to the infirmary. She kept a close eye on everything that came in or out of the villa. She checked on slave weavers and cooks; she surveyed the shepherds' work of milking the sheep and shearing them to make sure the number of fleeces matched the number of sheep. She patrolled for any cheating on the part of provisioners when they weighed out anything and everything. In the fields, foremen and overseers or the *vilicus* himself kept workers at their tasks and enforced discipline. The *vilicus*'s presence in the fields ensured that foremen performed their duties, and at the farmstead, he oversaw the work of his wife. He rewarded as well as punished, encouraged as well as scolded, and pitched in as well as watched. He shepherded his "flock" (*grex*) home at the end of the day. Inside the farmhouse, like the "attentive herdsman" (*diligens opilio*), he checked for injuries and illness (11.11.8). He inspected the workers' food and drink. The good *vilicus,* too, was supposed to act as a model for those in his charge. In the morning he briskly marched out at the head of the slaves, like a general (*dux*) leading "soldiers marching to some battle, with vigor and eagerness of mind" (11.1.17). He ate his meals in front of the other slaves, and, ideally, his behavior displayed an appropriate frugality.

The *vilicus* himself was subjected to his owner's gaze and supervision, and in a way that those under the authority of the *vilicus* would have seen. A delicate balance supported that authority yet made it clear the *vilicus* was not independent. Ideally, the landholder visited his estate often and announced more visits than he actually made to keep workers and *vilicus* in line. He inspected his land and watched for signs of lapsed discipline. He looked for missing vines, trees, produce, equipment, and slaves. Everything the *vilicus* did had to have the authorization of the owner: he could neither imprison nor free slaves from the *ergastulum,* undertake any business in the marketplace, buy or sell anything, or perform any sacrifice without the permission of the slaveholder or on his behalf. Only on holidays could the *vilicus* dine like a free man by lying on a couch. Moreover, the slaveholder himself talked to the slaves in the *vilicus*'s charge, chained and unchained, to inquire about their conditions; he himself checked their food, drink, and clothing. He often gave them the chance to complain about cruel or dishonest treatment. He punished rebels and workers who slandered their foremen, and he rewarded energetic and industrious slaves.

In general, Columella advocated a regime of control that extended beyond labor per se to slave workers' religious practices, social relations, movements, and bodies. As noted above, the *vilicus* was not supposed to perform any sacrifices except those authorized by his owner. He also forbade any contact with diviners and witches because in Columella's view they drove "ignorant people" (a category to which his slave laborers apparently belonged) to expend resources and to act in disgraceful ways. The taboo belonged to an attempt to regulate the social relations of his slave laborers including the *vilicus*. The latter could entertain no guests except his owner's friends and relations, nor should he allow visits from strangers unless such persons were friends of his master. He could not use his fellow slaves as a master to perform some service for himself, nor should he have intimate relations with them. He ate in their sight at his own table, and both he and they were supposed to eat around the household hearth and the master's guardian deity (probably a painting or statue). Presumably, their prescribed exhaustion at the end of the day limited the interactions that caused trouble, and, ideally, the relations encouraged at work were those of competition.

Chains and the *ergastulum* physically restrained the movement of recalcitrant slaves, and, as noted above, *vilicus* and *vilica* kept track of other slaves' comings and goings. In the ideal *villa rustica,* the *vilicus's* quarters were located so that he could observe his charges, and the farmstead itself was designed in a way that kept everyone as near as possible to make the *vilicus's* control of movement possible. No slave was supposed to leave the farm, and slave mobility on the farm was supposed to be limited by regulated paths, for one of the jobs of the *vilicus* was to see that slaves cut no new footpaths. If Columella's orders were followed, even the *vilicus* did not leave the estate except to find out something about farming, and he went to town or market only to buy or sell something for the estate.

Slaveholders like Columella even attempted to regulate the movement, body, and voice of the slave at work. The plowman serves as only one example that could be repeated in nearly every agricultural task discussed by Columella. After a meticulous description of oxen and how to yoke them, Columella instructs the plowman:

> The ploughman ... must walk on the broken ground and in every other furrow, must hold his plough slanted, running alternate furrows with the plough upright and at its full depth, but in such a way as not to leave anywhere any solid and unbroken ground. ... When the oxen come to a tree, he must keep them firmly in hand and check their pace. ... He should keep them in dread of his voice rather than of his lash, blows being his last resort when they balk at a task. He should never urge a bullock with a goad, for this makes him irritable and inclined to kick; yet he may urge him on now and then with a whip. (2.2.25–26, trans. E. S. Forster and E. H. Heffner, *LCL*)

Various other activities mandated control of the diet and sexual lives of slaves. Before attending to the bees, the beekeeper must not have sex, drink, or eat food with strong flavors like pickled fish, garlic and onions, and he had to wash because, according to Columella, bees hated dirt. Other authors held that bakers, cooks, and provisioners, too, could not have sex or drink before handling food or food containers. Those who had had sex were required to wash in a river or running water. Columella limited bathing to holidays, for in his view, frequent bathing detracted from physical strength. Above all the *vilicus* was forbidden to overindulge in drink, sleep, or sex.

Paternalism, the fatherly kindness and care of slaves, figured in the advice of the agricultural writers and made its imprint in the world of work. Columella consulted his slaves on a new task, so he could divine their abilities and make them more willing to perform. He talked to his well-behaved slaves in a friendly, familiar way because he believed this manner lightened their unending labor. In his view, the attention of owner and *vilicus* to the quality of the slave laborers' food and clothing contributed to a "justice and care" that increased the estate's productivity: it made better workers (1.8.19). Attending to the sick and tired, too, had a similar end in view: it nurtured in the recovered slave a good will and compliance that translated into more faithful service. Allowing slaves to make complaints introduced a sense that they had some appeal from their condition. Rewarding good slave laborers elevated them above their fellow slaves and encouraged them to identify with their owners and their aims through the awards of extra food, clothing, and rest for their diligence and hard work. In general, this was paternalistic logic at work: slaves were supposed to see their owner's actions as gifts – as boons, for which the return was slaves' labor, when in fact all of the "gifts" extracted slaves' labor and aimed to gain their willing submission in the production of the owner's income.

The response of slave men and women to these conditions will have varied with personality, rank, age, gender, and the specific practices of owners. Some no doubt acquiesced to paternalistic slaveholders and tried to make their way through a system of rewards and punishments. Others resisted openly and ended up in chains and the *ergastulum*. Many led lives somewhere in between. The last chapter gave a detailed list of slaves' acts of daily, low-level resistance that so dogged their owners. Here the point is how often these acts took place in the sphere of work. If we read slave owners' warnings, complaints, and practices as a response to slave behavior, and ignore owners' pejorative terms, we can glimpse how rural slaves might have gained time, space, and extra resources for themselves. Although they lacked the potential access to urban pleasures, rural slaves made their own ways around the estates following their own directions – hence the injunction to the *vilicus* to allow no new footpaths. In addition, Varro suggests that slaves had relations, friendly and hostile, with slaves on neighboring estates (1.15.1). Slaveholders' worries about slaves leaving the estate and their restraint on the *vilicus*'s visits to marketplace and town might have been well founded. The attempt to control laziness and to keep slave hands busy suggests that some slaves did in fact slow down the tempo of work or took control of it themselves. Slaves feigned illness or damaged tools to give themselves some time off.

Slave owners' warnings that the *vilicus* needed to keep foremen at their duties and their own careful oversight of the *vilicus* responded to slaveholders' distrust of slaves' ability to command without cruelty on the one side and laxness on the other. The gap between slave overseer and slave workers often may not have been as wide as slave owners desired. We can wonder whether the *vilicus* and his charges negotiated a regime of work that satisfied their own needs and interests at least within the conditions of their enslavement. Visits by the slaveholder, actual or promised, threatened to undo the slaves' own arrangements. Indeed, Columella himself saw the purpose of the slaveholder's visits as the inculcation of fear (*metus*) in both ordinary laborers and the *vilicus* himself (1.2.1).

It seems likely, too, that slaves appropriated more than the rewards handed out by their owners. Grain taken from the threshing room floor, missing fleeces at shearing time, sheep's milk that did not make it into the slaveholder's bucket – all suggest that slaves took for themselves some of the products of their labor, whether for their daily use or perhaps for trade. Some – the *vilicus, vilica,* foremen, and provisioners – had more opportunities. It seems likely that Columella insisted that the *vilicus* was a farmer not a trader – that he should buy and sell only on his owner's orders and should limit his visits to the local market or town – because some *vilici* disobeyed such rules. Certainly, such disobedient *vilici* could have done business only for themselves, but it is possible they also traded in products on behalf of their fellow slaves.

In the Urban Households of the Wealthy

In the city, slaves worked in the households of their wealthy owners: these slaves composed the *familia urbana* (the city household) mentioned at the beginning of the chapter. Law and literature attest to the importance of these slaves: in literature they appear as individuals in their own right and as background to the lives of the rich or famous, and in law they count as property of various sorts – bequest, gifts, and loans. Interestingly, work in the urban household seems to have been important to the slaves themselves. In the epitaphs and dedications from the city of Rome in which individuals have an occupational title, 73.8 percent of the slaves so identified worked in some thirty different households in the city (Table 2). More than 80 percent of these slaves provided various services for their owners, and it is on these slaves, and their freed colleagues, that this section focuses.

The occupations named in the epitaphs from the city of Rome show a wide range of services in the households of the wealthy (Table 1). The term "caretakers" in Table 1 refers to servants who took physical care of the house and its owner's possessions. Doorkeepers, the majordomo, men and women whose tasks involved cleaning and maintenance, and gardeners worked in specific areas of the house and its grounds. Other servants staffed the household infirmary. Slaves and freed slaves were also charged with the care of specific objects: in the epitaphs from Rome, we find a woman in charge of mirrors or a mirror holder (*Corpus of Latin Inscriptions* 6.7297), a pearl keeper (6.7884), clothes keepers and wardrobe guardians (6.6372, 6374, 33393, 33395, 7601), and clothes folders and pressers (6.7301, 9901). In some of these jobs, the maintenance of things overlapped with personal service. *Cubicularii*

51. Painting of an intimate scene, Villa Farnesina, Rome, late first century CE. The undressed man reclining on a couch and his bride, dressed and still wearing her veil, interact without regard to the servant, probably a *cubicularius* (bedchamber servant), who looks out at the viewer. The scene suggests the ways that certain domestic slaves were constantly present even in what we would regard as the most intimate or embarrassing moments in the lives of their owners (see Figures 54 and 55). (Photo Michael Larvey su concessione del Minstero per i Beni e le Attività Culturali – Soprintendenza Speciale per i Beni Archeologici di Roma)

(bedchamber servants) oversaw their masters' and patrons' bedrooms, controlled access to them, and were renowned as confidants (Figure 51). *Ornatrices* dressed hair and acted as personal maids (Figure 39); barbers cut hair and shaved household members. Masseurs or masseuses accompanied elite men or women to the baths. Doctors and midwives attended to their health. Some provisioned the household and were in charge of its stores. Cooks prepared meals, served by waiters, carvers, and wine pourers (Figures 52–53). Musicians, actors, and readers entertained owner and guests. Litter bearers carried the master and mistress when they went out, accompanied by attendants. At home and outside, foot servants waited – available for small tasks and errands like

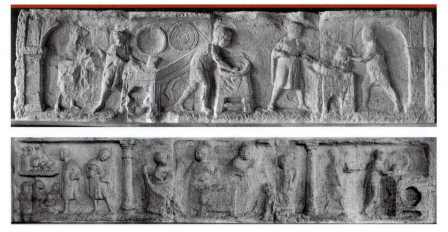

52. Friezes of cooks, waiters, and clean-up crew, Trier. (Photo Rheinisches Landesmuseum, Trier)

the female servant in Figure 70. Outside of the imperial household, only the rich and powerful Statilii had bodyguards who identified their work.

Slaveholders also enjoyed having slave children called *delicia* hanging around on a variety of occasions. Although not a job per se, these *delicia* were diversion, entertainment, and pleasant scenery. Child nurses took care of the physical needs of babies and young children; child attendants escorted their charges to school and kept a general watch over their activities. Some were assigned care of the household's slave children. Slave and freed financial managers, accountants, and agents kept accounts, handled disbursements, and dealt with the day-to-day management of property. Secretaries wrote letters and took dictation. The men in social organization dealt with outsiders and kept order within the household. Some in this category were announcers (*nomenclatores*) who accompanied their owners, telling them the names of individuals they encountered.

Although this section focuses on slaves and ex-slaves who provided various services, a complete picture of *familia urbana* must at least mention builders and artisans associated with elite households. The Statilii, for example, had their own construction staff: it seems likely that they also worked on buildings other than the family's houses, since

53. Mosaic of varieties of servants, Thugga, mid-late third century CE. The mosaic distinguishes slaves by their dress, grooming, and activities. Two very large slaves, simply dressed, carry amphorae and pour wine into bowls held out by two younger, groomed, and well-dressed servants. At each side of the mosaic, two even younger attendants with long hair hold other accoutrements for a banquet – a bunch of roses and spray of myrtle (?) and a towel and a jug. (Courtesy Katherine M. D. Dunbabin)

the Statilii had an amphitheater and warehouses. Slave women in the household spun wool; slave men cleaned and processed it along with the household's dirty clothes. Tailors and menders made and mended clothes. Last, following a common requirement of class and good taste, the household had its own bakers.

As in the countryside, gender and age counted. In the Statilian household and others, slave women worked at a variety of tasks. Spinners were invariably slave women, and women also made and mended clothing. Slave and freed women appear as different kinds of personal servants – foot servants and attendants, maids and hairdressers. As noted above, enslaved women took care of mirrors, jewelry, and clothing. Child nurses and some child minders/attendants of elite children were slaves or freed women. Midwives and women with the title *medica* attended to their owners' health and probably to the pregnancies and illnesses of slave women in the *familia*. Slave women and

Table 1. Service Occupations in the Large Domestic
Household (Includes Slaves and Freed Slaves)

Occupation	Individuals	Distinct Job Titles
Teachers	2	2
Architects and surveyors	4	3
Doctors and midwives	22[a]	2
Barbers and hairdressers	11[a]	2
Masseurs and oilers	8[a]	1
Readers and entertainers	10[a]	7
Bath attendants	4	2
Child nurses and attendants	34[a]	5
Bodyguards	10	2
Room servants	57[a]	11
Table servants	2	1
Cooks	9	1
Provisioners	11	4
Caretakers	22[a]	10
Gardeners	5	3
Social organizers	9	4
Animal tenders	7	6
Runners and bearers	26	3
Financial agents	54	8
Administrators	50	15
Secretaries and copyists	28[a]	6
Total	385	98

[a] Includes women.

Adapted from Joshel (1992: p. 75, table 3.2).

freedwomen acted as readers and secretaries, although they, unlike their male counterparts, did not administer the household's property, finances, or public business.

Other evidence indicates that work began in childhood as early as age five (*Digest* 7.7.6.1). From apprenticeship contracts from Egypt, the legal sources, and literature, we know that slaves were often trained in childhood for their jobs: some learned weaving, smithing, or hairdressing, some music, and others reading, writing, and mathematics. In large households, slave boys and girls were often trained for work in their owner's own domestic establishments, and in others, they were trained to be sold – that is, as an investment for their owners. Large domestic households, like Pliny's (*Letters* 7.27.13), had a *paedagogium*, a school or training establishment for the household's slave children.

Without proper servants, a person of substance or someone with aspirations to social standing could not live nobly (Figure 53). Cicero, for example, criticized the senator Lucius Calpurnius Piso not only for the bad food and wine served at his dinner table but also for his lack of proper servants (*Against Piso* 67). Dirty slaves waited on Piso's guests, and some of them were old, not young and attractive. His cook doubled as the hall porter, and he had no bakers, so he served bread bought in the market. Men and women of taste and class had proper waiters, wine pourers, cooks, provisioners, attendants, bedchamber servants, hairdressers, and masseurs to take care of their physical needs. When important men went out in the city, servants as well as clients accompanied them; attendants, too, escorted wealthy women. Travel meant an entourage of attendants, litter bearers, and runners. Accountants, secretaries, or agents kept accounts, handled monies, and took care of the day-to-day management of property. Whether it was the man of standing like Piso who was shamed by sloppy, inappropriate servants or the social upstart who was ridiculed for deriving his sense of self-importance from a crowd of waiters and maids, the assumption was the same: the person of substance required servants.

The large number of these servants must be connected with the significance of slaves as a constituent of wealth. The prefect of Rome in 61 CE supposedly had four hundred servants living under his roof. In the reign of Augustus, men sent into exile could take only twenty servants – a number meant to be punitive. When Seneca was traveling simply, he took what to him was *only* one cartful of slaves (*Letters* 87.2). In his novel, Petronius pokes fun at the rich, vulgar freedman Trimalchio and his horde of waiters, cooks, bath attendants, runners, and litter bearers. Yet the point remains: proper servants alone were not sufficient – men or women of standing were measured by the number of their attendants and litter bearers. Like precious inanimate objects, these slave men and women counted as "things" that displayed the wealth and status of their owners. Further, their assigned tasks made them *visible* as wealth to guest, onlooker, and owner.

Domestic servants not only labored under a regime that made them a display of their owners' wealth and importance, they also acted as what we might see as "middlemen" in the relations between their owners and their clients or less important guests. The satirist Juvenal, for example, complains about the treatment of poor clients (esp. *Satires* 5.24 ff.). Wealthy men assign the least attractive and most inappropriate slaves to wait on them, while their own special servants refuse to serve these unimportant guests. In effect, slaves, not their owners, put clients in their place, and the rich were elevated without direct involvement in their clients' humiliation. Poor clients visited their frustration on slaves and avoided a direct confrontation with their social betters, whom they could not afford to alienate. All the tensions in the unequal relations of rich and poor were directed toward the servant.

Quite literally, domestic servants also acted as doors and walls. Roman authors express disdain for snobby doorkeepers: the latter refuse visitors' entrance to their owners' houses, turn away the unimportant, or must be tipped. The houses of the wealthy were not strictly divided between public and private rooms; rather, areas of common access like the atrium gave way to other areas, dining rooms and bedrooms, to which only certain chosen guests were invited. Various servants directed the movement and access of visitors. The historian Andrew Wallace-Hadrill calls them "living barriers to access to the master" (1994: 39).

Columella's claims about the leisure of urban slaves introduce questions about the work life of these servants, the shape of the working day, and their freedom of movement. Job titles seem to imply that some slaves had time on their hands: What did a litter bearer do when his owner had no place to go, walked, or spent four hours at his destination? What did the foot servant do when her mistress was taking a nap? What did the waiter do when no meal was served? The daily schedule of the elite certainly kept their servants busy. As in the country, the day began early in the city, at around six in the summer and seven in the winter. Common practice until the middle of the first century CE required that the household slaves greet their owners at the beginning of the day. After dressing, shaving, and eating a light breakfast, the master held his morning reception of friends and clients (*salutatio*) and then went to the forum or courts; after a light lunch and a siesta in the summer, he made a trip to the baths. For the mistress, morning brought a trip to the baths, her toilette, visits with friends, and her own business affairs. All of these activities required the labor of servants. The slaveholder's children were tended, the boys escorted to school by slaves or freed slaves. Meanwhile, slave and freed stewards, agents, and administrators attended to their master's property and financial matters. Last but not least, there was dinner either at home or outside. The former might mean a dinner party that engaged the energies of cook, waiters, entertainers, foot servants, and clean-up crew; the latter meant attendants and often litter bearers.

Although it would seem that some servants had time on their hands at certain times of the day, for many, waiting around, being on hand, was part of their work (Figures 54–55). Thus, slaveholders' leisure meant their slaves' labor. For others, nurses, *cubicularii,* and maids, work had no time limits. As noted in the last chapter, nurses slept with their charges, personal servants in their owners' bedrooms or at their doors. Moreover, Roman literature offers many instances of slaveholders' demands breaching established schedules of work and leisure time and even what we might see as the definition of the job. In Seneca's portrayal of a night owl named Sextus Papinius, the slave owner's demands, however unreasonable, trumped any other activity – even sleep (*Moral Letters* 122.15–16). Papinius got up around 8:00 p.m. and began his "day" by punishing slaves. At midnight, he exercised his voice. At 2:00 a.m., he went out for a drive. At dawn, after his bath, the waiters and attendants, cooks and provisioners scrambled to serve their master, who now wanted his dinner.

For Seneca, the problem with Papinius's lifestyle was his nocturnal schedule, not the frantic efforts of his slaves. Seneca criticized slave owners' cruelty and the lowliness of their slaves' labor, but he accepted

54. Painting from the House of the Chaste Lovers (IX.12.6–7), Pompeii. This painting and the painting in Figure 55, like that from the Villa Farnesina (Figure 51), depict servants at the edge of their owners' lives. The two men, each accompanied by a woman, languish in various states of drunkenness. The man at the right has passed out, and a female servant fans him, apparently attempting to wake him. (Photo Michael Larvey su concessione del Minstero per i Beni e le Attività Culturali – Soprintendenza Speciale per i Beni Archeologici di Napoli e Pompei)

the pattern of pleasing as a sort of common sense – the requirement that the slaveholder's demands should take precedence. Even upstanding, conservative Roman slaveholders claimed their servants' time and energies. In a letter written in the early second century CE, Pliny the Younger catalogs the long list of his uncle's books, written despite the demands of a busy public life (*Letters* 3.5). His uncle's habits explain how he was able to accomplish all this: he would get up in the middle

55. Painting from the House of the Chaste Lovers (IX.12.6–7), Pompeii. See
the comment on Figure 54. At the left, the woman with a mantle pulled over
her head prepares to leave, although she still has a drinking cup in her hand.
Apparently, she is very drunk, for a young servant has to hold her up. If she is
at the margins of the drinking figures in the central scene, her slave attendant is
even more marginal still. (Photo Michael Larvey su concessione del Minstero per
i Beni e le Attività Culturali – Soprintendenza Speciale per i Beni Archeologici
di Napoli e Pompei)

of the night, work after dinner, and devote every minute on any journey to work. Pliny the Elder's practices required the same schedule
of his slaves. When he napped or dined, a servant read to him; if he
dictated his writings in the hours after dinner, he called on the services
of a secretary; and when he traveled, he had a stenographer by his side
along with book and writing tablets.

In effect, the working life of servants was shaped by their proximity to their owners. Physical closeness and in some cases intimacy

evoked the affection of the owner with consequent benefits to the slave – good treatment, kindness, and even the boon of manumission. Roman senators from Cicero to Pliny testify to their warm regards for slaves that often translated into freedom for the slave. As noted in Chapter 1, Cicero and his family loved Cicero's secretary Tiro and greeted his manumission with joy. Pliny the Younger worried about the illness of his slaves and mourned their deaths (*Letters* 8.16; 8.19). He fretted about his slave reader Encolpius when dust caused him to spit up blood. He insisted that he stop his literary activities and placed him in the care of doctors (*Letters* 8.1). Pliny sent his ailing freedman Zosimus, a reader, actor, and musician, to Egypt for his health when he began to spit blood, and when the illness returned after too many days of work, he sent him to the estate of a friend and colleague where the air was healthy: he asked that his staff ("your people") take him in and cover his expenses (*Letters* 5.19). Perhaps this affection and care, as well as Zosimus's talent on which Pliny comments, resulted in Zosimus's freedom. However, that freedom did not mean autonomy for Tiro or for Zosimus – in part because of their occupations and in part because of their owners' desire to hold on to the services they provided.

The epitaphs of servants from the city of Rome indicate that many slaves were freed. In every field, some slaves attained their freedom (Table 2). Yet these epitaphs tell us only about slaves and freed slaves who noted their job titles. In reality, exactly how many slaves were freed and in which occupations is difficult to calculate because most epitaphs do not name the occupations of the deceased and their com-memorators, and those individuals, too, worked. Moreover, some of the slaves with occupational titles died before they changed jobs. Foot servants (*pedisequii*), for example, tended to be slaves, but where we have ages at death, we can observe that most died in their teens and early twenties before, perhaps, they took up other duties.

Cicero and Pliny give us only one side of the relationship, and we can at least wonder about the other side. They may have accurately recounted the feelings and behavior of their slaves and freed-men; however, these slaveholders imagined that their valued slaves

Table 2. Occupations of Slaves, Freed Slaves, and Freeborn Romans

Occupation Group	Legal Status					
	Slave	Uncertain Slave	Freedman	Freeborn	Uncertain Freeborn	Total
Building	19 (4.1)	7 (3.4)	30 (7.1)	10 (23.3)	46 (13.9)	112 (7.6)
Manufacture	52 (11.1)	25 (12.2)	147 (34.9)	8 (18.6)	99 (29.8)	331 (22.5)
Sales	3 (0.6)	5 (2.4)	46 (10.9)	8 (18.6)	46 (13.9)	108 (7.3)
Banking	—	—	28 (6.7)	1 (2.3)	13 (3.9)	42 (2.9)
Professional service	15 (3.2)	11 (5.4)	35 (8.3)	5 (11.6)	54 (16.3)	120 (8.2)
Skilled service	37 (7.9)	12 (5.9)	13 (3.1)	2 (4.7)	11 (3.3)	75 (5.1)
Domestic service	129 (27.5)	77 (37.6)	85 (20.2)	2 (4.7)	28 (8.4)	321 (21.8)
Transportation	32 (6.8)	11 (5.4)	8 (1.9)	1 (2.3)	3 (0.9)	55 (3.7)
Administration	182 (38.8)	57 (27.8)	29 (6.9)	6 (14.0)	32 (9.6)	306 (20.8)
Total	469 (100)	205 (100)	421 (100)	43 (100)	332 (100)	1,470 (100)

Note: Figures in parentheses are percentages.
Adapted from Joshel (1992: p. 127, table 5.2).

shared their owners' experience. According to Pliny, the illness of his reader Encolpius was sad for them both: "who will read my books and love them (as he does)? To whom will I listen (with such attention)?" (*Letters* 8.1). The slave's feelings and interests supposedly mirrored his owner's. If Encolpius was not the docile dependent that Pliny depicts, then we might glimpse the self-control required by this slave reader in Pliny's account. If Pliny behaved as he portrayed himself in his letters, he would have talked on and on about his various endeavors. Encolpius could not simply close the book, so to speak, as we can, when bored or irritated by Pliny's constant talk about himself. If, in contrast to what Pliny assumed, Encolpius's entire self was not bound up with Pliny's literary projects, he had to rein in his boredom, frustration, or irritation to act in the way his owner observed.

Regardless of the slaveholder's affection, proximity created discomfort and posed certain dangers to the slave. Slave owners like Columella talked more familiarly with their rural slaves than their urban staff because, they believed, it lightened their heavier workload. In such cases, domestic servants waited on an owner who maintained his distance. In part, the picture of slaves in literature made them scenery;

like houses and furnishings, they were simply there (see Figures 51 and 54–55). Often the services of these slaves were obscured in expressions like "a book was read" or "a bath was taken," and, instead of instances of slaves performing tasks, the author simply noted the slave owner's orders. How, we might ask, did slaves experience their own transparency? How did they deal with treatment that was neither violent nor kind but simply ignored their constant presence except as the recipients of orders, and even then, as tools useful for particular tasks?

Proximity also put slaves in the urban household closer to the slaveholder's whip. In the common view of slaveholders, their ability to create fear in their slaves was important for gaining good service: constant fear of corporal punishment kept the servant in line. Every order came with the implicit threat of punishment for failure, real or imagined. As we have seen, Roman literature is full of episodes of slaveholders punishing their servants. Moreover, when Seneca urged slave owners to exert *self*-control, he suggests how their irritation about unrelated matters was easily redirected to the slave (*On Anger* 3.32.1). Ever present and nearby, house servants were ever available to command and within easy reach of a moody owner: avoiding the whip as well as the hope of reward made obedience, at least for some, necessary.

Last but not least is the question of slave servants' ability to move about the city that provided pleasure and entertainments not available in the countryside. The work of some room attendants and personal servants kept them within the confines of the house or at their owners' sides. When litter bearers had delivered their owner to his or her destination, it seems doubtful that they were then free to wander the streets or visit taverns. Even accompanying their owners to the games could limit slaves' enjoyment, if they were supposed to be at hand to serve. Assigned tasks often took others outside the house: for example, managers of warehouses (*horrearii*) to the warehouses and rent collectors and superintendents (*insularii*) to apartment buildings or blocks of flats. Messengers sent to deliver a letter or foot servants sent on errands went out into the city, and in law we hear complaints that some slaves loitered on errands or "indulge(d) in aimless roaming and, after wasting time on trivialities, return(ed) home at a late hour" (*Digest* 21.1.1.1; 21.1.17.14). Evidently, some domestic slaves enjoyed the city during work hours.

On certain holidays, like the Saturnalia and the Compitalia in December and early January, slaves had time to celebrate with each other and to visit the sights, although at least for the Saturnalia, celebrations took place in the house and often involved the slaveholder. We know little about the rest of the time. Beyond the observation of Columella, other evidence suggests that slave men, at least, were customers of the city's taverns and brothels, but when these visits took place is not clear. We know that slaves could visit the baths, if they had the fee, and attended the games, if they could get tickets.

Some slaveholders may have limited the movements of their urban slaves. In Petronius's satire of the vulgar freedman Trimalchio, the novel's narrator observes a sign on the door of Trimalchio's house: "Any slave who goes out without the master's permission will receive one hundred lashes" (28.7). How to interpret this piece of evidence is difficult. First, such a sign presumes slave literacy – certainly the case for some slaves but not all. Second, since it was posted on the front door, its audience would seem to be guests and visitors, not the slaves inside, and so it displays to outsiders the power of Trimalchio as slaveholder. Last but not least, one hundred lashes would break even the strongest back, if they did not kill the slave. Nonetheless, the exaggeration here may not be the control of slave movement but the way the gauche Trimalchio practices it and shows off his power to visitors.

Slave and freed supervisors on the staff no doubt oversaw the work of other slaves and kept track of their movements, but we know less about them than their counterparts in the imperial household, where we can trace the development of supervision. Moreover, we have no set of instructions for supervisors on the urban staff like those laid out in the agricultural manuals for the foremen and *vilicus* in the country. Nonetheless, job titles in inscriptions and passages in law and literature give us some idea of who watched whom. The *paedagogus puerorum* directed the household's slave children. The *supra lecticarios* managed other litter bears. A doorkeeper (*ostiarius*) stationed at the front door knew who left and who returned. In the early second century BCE, the *atriensis* was a majordomo of sorts, although later the title was used for ordinary cleaners. In some houses, a chief *cubicularius* (bedchamber servant), often a freed slave, was in charge of other personal servants. Last, the *dispensator* was a chief steward, although we know most about his financial activities. In the household of the Statilii, the *dispensator* Titus Statilius Auctus had his own slaves and at least by the end of his career became a freedman (*Corpus of Latin Inscriptions* 6.6266, 6268, 6385, 6398, 6474); other *dispensatores* were slaves, yet slaves with their own slaves (*vicarii*). As for slaves in the country, the distance between slave overseers and their underlings remains a question: Did supervisors and their charges negotiate work, its pace, and slave movement in and out of the household?

In elite households, hundreds of lives and variations were shaped by age, gender, and occupation – especially by its responsibilities, needed skills, and proximity to owners. Some of the acts of daily, low-level resistance mentioned in Chapter 4 were enacted specifically at work. As noted above, servants sent on various errands set their own pace and used the time that slave owners claimed for their own uses – visiting, wandering, perusing the shops; accountants cooked the books; and others appropriated food stuffs or took for their own items of the slaveholder's property, although in the case of costly goods, the "theft" was often connected with flight. Slaveholders' complaints about quick-tempered, silly, obstinate, sluggish slaves bespeak slaves' refusal to serve with complete subservience. Where slaves worked in proximity to their owners, where contact was daily and often continuous, in the most intimate of physical spaces, these behaviors would have been more immediately noticeable and, at the same time, more immediately irritating to the slaveholder or satisfying to the slave.

The large proportion of slave men and women whose job titles identify them as various sorts of servants in the epitaphs from the city of Rome raises questions about accommodation and resistance: What did it mean to claim this labor? In Roman literature, servants appear as scenery or as those who merely cater to the physical demands of their owners. Judged in these terms, the epitaphs of slave servants would seem to define their work as the satisfaction of the needs of others. Such a reading, however, adopts the perspective of the slaveholder, who saw all domestic work as a form of pleasing. Servants themselves did not necessarily share this view.

Modern Roman historians have argued about meanings of servants' job titles. Some read them as claims to rank in a domestic hierarchy. Others see these slaves' job titles as indications of associations and links within the community of slaves composed of the household's slaves and ex-slaves. Others read slaves' pride in their work, although it is not clear if such pride meant accommodation to the master's view or a different standard. Considering the epitaphs of domestic slaves in terms of their position in the relations of server and served opens up other interpretations that suggest a daily mundane resistance grounded in the experience of slavery itself.

The very use of job titles in epitaphs records how slaves and freed slaves maintained slaveholders and their property – cooking, serving, dressing, attending children and adults, reading, taking notes, keeping accounts, cleaning, repairing house and furniture. In all these ways, domestics produced for their owners a life of leisure appropriate to their social standing. Yet as pointed out in the last chapter, paternalistic slaveholders saw their slaves, not themselves, as dependent. Slave testimony from the American South makes it clear that slaves themselves saw through slaveholders' views that defined them as helpless and indulged and found satisfaction in their owners' passivity. Roman slaves did not leave such articulate records, but perhaps their occupational titles suggest a similar awareness. Where, for example, slave owners ignored the waiter or saw his actions as expressions of their own power and position, the waiter could see that mistress and master did not fetch their own meals. At least, the job titles of domestic servants name their own activity and slaveholders' passivity in daily tasks: they did what their owners could not do without losing social standing. In effect, in these areas the slaveholder was dependent on the slave, not vice versa.

Since slaveholders reduced domestic work to pleasing, they could read accommodation in the use of these job titles, not rebellion or even recalcitrance. However, a message about their dependence was there to be read by fellow slaves and ex-slaves who visited the tomb to bury and honor their family and friends and who lived similar experiences in the same household.

Most historians agree that in many ways the opportunities for a better life were greater in the city. Indeed, banishment to the country was considered a punishment. Where law deals with slaves' *peculia,* the jurists speak of resources and monies that stem from urban activities. Roman authors indicate the possibility of accumulating tips and material rewards. Slave epitaphs from the city of Rome indicate that some slaves, at least, had their own slaves (*vicarii*). In general, urban slaves had greater opportunities for manumission. Last, but not least, in the city (beyond the "follies" mentioned by Columella), urban slaves would find other slaves working in other households and the city's shops and markets.

In the Marketplace: Shop and Workshop

Urban slaves who did not work in the households of the elite belonged to a variety of owners – freeborn and freed, rich businesspeople and artisans of middling income, and they worked in conditions as varied as the commercial landscape of the city. Small shops, larger establishments like bakeries and fulleries, temporary booths in open spaces and designated marketplaces all sold, made, or processed various items for sale – foodstuffs, jewelry and luxury items, clothes and cloth, furniture and household goods. Bars, taverns, and brothels provided drink, food, entertainment, and sex. In the streets, at the baths, and around the amphitheater and theater, hawkers offered food, drink, and various items, agricultural and manufactured. At least as far as we can tell from the Roman port of Ostia and the city of Pompeii, the Romans did not separate shops, workshops, and markets from purely residential

56. House of the Large Portal (V.35), Herculaneum. (Courtesy of Andrew Wallace-Hadrill)

areas, although some areas, especially along the major streets, often were crowded with shops. Anyone who left a fancy house often found a shop or two flanking the front door (Figure 56). Continuing down the street, they could well have passed other shops, workshops, and peddlers selling various goods door-to-door.

In literature, law, inscriptions, reliefs, and paintings, we find slaves in nearly every nondomestic activity. The following discussion, however, surveys sales and production. Yet it should be noted, this focus omits two places where slave women worked and found themselves especially vulnerable – taverns and brothels (Figures 57–60). For workshops and shops outside of these two venues, we can look at the conditions of work and then observe the implications for the lives of slave participants.

Slaves were the labor force in larger establishments like bakeries and fulleries. The work of milling grain and baking bread began before dawn and continued for long hours. A mule, often directed by a worker, turned the millstone; slaves gathered the flour from the mill,

57. Tavern of Vetutius Placidus (I.8.9), Pompeii. Taverns and bars of various sorts served food and drink to customers who were usually from the lower classes including slaves. Sunk into the counter are large containers probably filled with various snacks – dried beans, fruit, chickpeas. Jars on the floor or on racks held wine. The right-hand wall has a *lararium* with a painting that depicts the guardian spirit (*genius*) of the proprietor, Bacchus (god of wine), and Mercury (patron god of money making). (Photo Antonia Mulas)

turned the machines that kneaded the dough, formed the dough into loaves, and placed them in the ovens (Figure 61). Working conditions were unpleasant, to say the least: in many bakeries slaves labored in the dark, and in heat; the smoke from the ovens irritated eyes and blackened faces; flour dust covered bodies (no wonder, as we have seen in Chapter 4, slaves were sent to mills as punishment).

We can only speculate about relations among the workers, although the friezes from the tomb of Eurysaces (Figure 61) depict the cooperative efforts needed in particular tasks. It seems unlikely that, at least during working hours, they participated in the colorful life of the street. Some workers lived in or near the work areas themselves, so the space of "home" and "work" overlapped. In some cities, *collegia* of bakers provided moments of bakerly camaraderie. Often translated as guild, an occupational *collegium* was less like a medieval guild that regulated technical practices and personnel and more like a club or self-help society: its

58. Painting from the Tavern (*Caupona*) of Salvius (VI.14.35), Pompeii. Barmaids, often slave women, were frequently subject to rough treatment and pawing by the bar's male customers; some worked as part-time prostitutes. In this painting, however, according to John Clarke (2003, pp. 165–67), the woman is in control. Two male customers argue about who gets the wine carried by the waitress: the man on the left calls out "Here!" (*hoc*), and the one on the right "No! It's mine! (*non mia est*). The waitress, much larger than the two men, first answers, "Whoever wants it, take it" (*qui vol, sumat*) and then, "Oceanus, come and drink! (*Oceane, veni bibe*). Clarke argues that her response shifts from indifference to aggression: he suggests that she calls on the toughest guy in the bar to settle the contest (Oceanus was the name of a famous Pompeiian gladiator) or that by calling them Oceanus she makes fun of their manliness. Either way, the humor of the painting aims to turn the usual order upside down: the waitress controls the male customer, not the other way around. (Photo Michael Larvey su concessione del Minstero per i Beni e le Attività Culturali – Soprintendenza Speciale per i Beni Archeologici di Napoli e Pompei)

59. Large brothel (VII.12.18), Pompeii. (Photo Michael Larvey su concessione del Minstero per i Beni e le Attività Culturali – Soprintendenza Speciale per i Beni Archeologici di Napoli e Pompei)

richer members provided feasts, celebrations, and often burial space for the ordinary laborers like the men in Eurysaces's bakery, about whom we know little. In addition, besides the usual holidays for slaves, during the Vestalia in honor of Vesta, bakeries closed and bakers feasted from June 7 to 15. Whatever their participation in the feasts, ordinary workers seem to have had a week's break from work.

Those who owned or ran the bakeries, and were often the officers of the bakers' *collegium,* were another matter. The huge and elaborate tomb of Marceius Vergilius Eurysaces, baker and contractor, monumentalizes his business and indicates his wealth (Figure 62). Less wealthy but successful were Publius Nonius Zethus and his wife and fellow ex-slave, Nonia Pelagia, from Ostia (Figure 63). Zethus belonged to the *Augustales,* a group whose members, often freedmen, funded public projects and participated in the imperial cult. The marble block on

60. Interior of large brothel (VII.12.18), Pompeii.
(a) Prostitutes, often slaves, worked in small rooms, sometimes with masonry beds, as in this brothel. (b) Here a corridor of such rooms has paintings of sexual scenes above the door. (Photo Michael Larvey su concessione del Minstero per i Beni e le Attività Culturali – Soprintendenza Speciale per i Beni Archeologici di Napoli e Pompei)

(a)

(b)

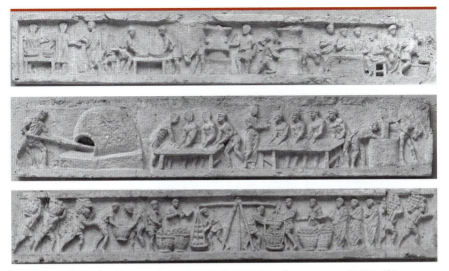

61. Frieze from the Tomb of Eurysaces, Rome, late first century BCE. (Singer, Neg. D-DAI-ROM 1972.3819, 1972.3826, 1972.3827)

which they put their epitaph provided space for eight cinerary urns for family, freedmen, or slaves (which we do not know). On each side of their epitaph, they depicted scenes from their bakery. We would like to know how these ex-slaves came by their bakery: Were they originally workers? Had they managed the bakery for an ex-master? Or, perhaps, as suggested by other cases recounted in the *Digest,* their master/ex-master left them the bakery in his will.

The same gap between owners/managers and laborers, too, characterized fulleries, commercial laundries of new cloth and already-worn clothing. Fullers were targets of Roman authors who depicted them as vulgar and stained by the nature of fulling practices, yet it is evident that some attained wealth. For their laborers, the work was hard, the working conditions miserable. Rather than dry and dusty like the bakery, the fullery was damp and smelly, primarily from the use of water, detergents, and degreasers that included urine, human and animal. Leaning on sidewalls of tubs, workers trod on clothes or cloth in a mixture of water and detergent made of various substances – nitron, potash, soapwort, or urine (Figures 64–66). Slave feet took the place of the automated movement of the modern washing machine, performing

62. Tomb of Marceius Vergilius Eurysaces, Rome, late first century BCE. (Alinari/Art Resource, New York)

63. Sarcophagus of Publius Nonius Zethus, first century CE. (Photo Vatican Museums)

64. Stele of a fuller, Sens. (Cl. J.-P. Elie, Musées de Sens)

65. Tubs from the Fullery of Stephanus (I.6.7), Pompeii. (su concessione del Ministero per i Beni e le Attività Culturali – Soprintendenza Speciale per i Beni Archeologici di Napoli e Pompei)

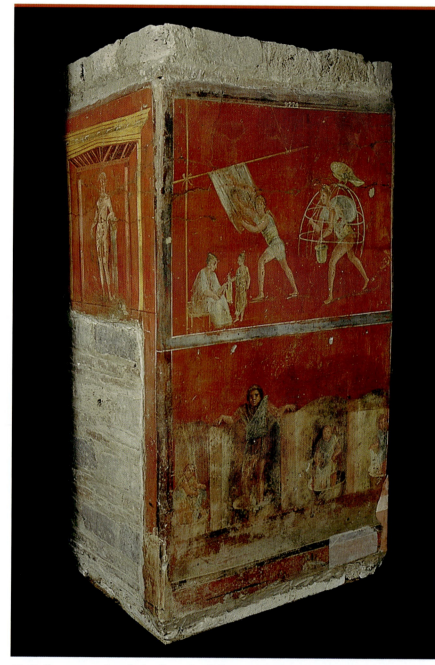

66. Fullers on a painted pier from the fullery at VI.8.20, Pompeii. (Photo Michael Larvey su concessione del Minstero per i Beni e le Attività Culturali – Soprintendenza Speciale per i Beni Archeologici di Napoli e Pompei)

67. Scene of a fullers' *collegium*, Fullery of Primus (VI.14.21–22), Pompeii. (Courtesy W. M. Jongman)

what was called the "fullers' jump" (Figure 64). Workers rinsed the material, beat it to tighten it, and then hung it to dry. They brushed it to treat the nap and then hung it on wicker frames under which they burned sulphur to whiten it (Figure 66). Workers rubbed the clothes with various kinds of "fuller's earth" – concoctions that produced different effects. Some restored color; others made them white and shiny – as, for example, those used for the togas of candidates standing for election. Mark Bradley points out that the working conditions were not only unpleasant but also unhealthy (2002). Feet that spent long hours in water were susceptible to infection; working with urine and fuller's earth caused various skin irritations and rashes; and breathing burning sulphur perhaps meant persistent respiratory problems.

Fullers belonged to *collegia,* but, as with bakers, we are best informed about the activities of the wealthier men who held office in the *collegia.* Holidays and public festivals, too, brought breaks in fullers' arduous working regime. Most important for fullers was the Quinquatrus on March 19. The holiday in honor of Minerva, patron goddess of fullers and other craftsmen, meant five days of feasting,

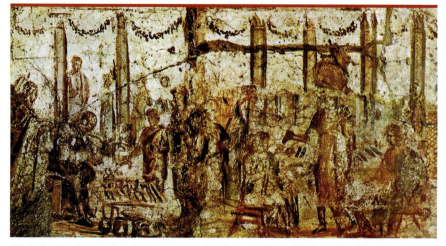

68. Sales in the marketplace, painting in the Praedia of Julia Felix (II.4.3), Pompeii. (Photo Michael Larvey su concessione del Minstero per i Beni e le Attività Culturali – Soprintendenza Speciale per i Beni Archeologici di Napoli e Pompei)

although quite surprising to us, these feasts took place in the fullery itself (Figure 67).

Managers of some bakeries and fulleries may well have been *institores,* agents appointed by the owner to run the business. The term covers a wide range of activities: management, sales, and deliveries. The legal sources make it clear that men and women, boys and girls, and slaves and free persons acted as *institores,* but often both in law and in literature the *institor* was a slave. Some had a temporary booth or spot at the weekly market or in designated marketplaces like those selling goods in the painting from the rental property of Julia Felix in Pompeii (Figure 68). Peddlers often figured in this category. They moved from place to place, selling their goods. Some worked for tailors and cloth merchants, hawking and selling clothes and cloth from door to door (*Digest* 14.3.4); some sold bread, sent by the baker to a particular location (14.3.5.9); some made their way from one upper-class house to another (14.3.4). Others sold pastries, sweets, and sausages in the street and in the baths at the peak hour of bathing. They called out their offerings in loud voices – a source of complaint to those who wanted some peace and quiet. The jurists focused on the financial responsibility

69. Shop/tavern at the House of Neptune and Amphitrite (V.6), Herculaneum. (Photo Michael Larvey su concessione del Minstero per i Beni e le Attività Culturali – Soprintendenza Speciale per i Beni Archeologici di Napoli e Pompei)

of peddler-*institores* for monies and goods; Roman authors use them as scenery or complain about their noisy cries. We might wonder about the working lives of slave peddlers who spent the day on their feet, moved among bathers at the baths, or made their way from fancy house to fancy house. We can only speculate about their knowledge of the city, their participation in street life, and their relations with other slaves encountered on their rounds.

Whether as managers or as laborers, slave men and women worked in the shops of the city, which often were also workshops where goods were made as well as sold. Most were small, and production itself was on a small scale. The typical shop had a wide opening to the street and a back room for storage, production, or living quarters; in some cases, the remains of stairs suggest a room on the second floor for artisan, family, and perhaps a slave or two (Figure 69). At Pompeii, the presence of tools, equipment, or shop signs indicates the kind of goods produced, but most often we have only the bare bones of the work space, and in either case we must rely on paintings and reliefs to give us an idea of the work and its environment. With few exceptions, however, we do not know if the retailers and artisans depicted represent slaves, ex-slaves, or freeborn citizens.

70. Relief of a cushion and cloth shop, Rome, now Florence, mid-first century CE. (Scala/Art Resource, New York)

A relief of a cushion and cloth shop originally from Rome (mid-first century CE) shows the outlines of a shop with a tiled roof held by two columns: the front room, at least, easily accommodates seven people (Figure 70). Inside, a bar that hangs over workers and customers displays cushions and pieces of cloth. Two men hold up a piece of cloth for two customers – a seated couple: he wears a toga, and she the dress of a proper Roman woman. Behind them, a female servant dressed in a tunic waits in attendance: she is perhaps the foot servant of the seated woman. Two other men in tunics stand on each side of the central group. The men in tunics apparently were workers and/or salesmen; here they cater to their upper-class customers, who sit and ponder the goods brought out for them.

A well-known relief from Ostia, perhaps even a shop sign, depicts another venue and experience of the marketplace (Figure 71). A saleswoman, dressed in a simple tunic, with a plain hairdo and without jewelry, hands a piece of fruit to a customer dressed in cloak and boots

71. Relief of a saleswomen of poultry and fruit (?), Ostia, late second century CE. (Courtesy Fototeca Unione)

(whose size has more to do with the composition of the relief than his social status); with her other hand, she grasps another piece of fruit (?) on a platter. Behind her, we glimpse the head of a person whose role and even gender is unclear – perhaps he or she was an assistant. The saleswoman's counter is composed of cages holding birds (chickens?) and rabbits. The baskets stacked next to her may have held snails, one of which hangs in the empty space beside her. Two birds, already butchered, hang from a bar to the left, and two monkeys, evidently pets, sit on the counter to the right. On the left, two other bearded men, also dressed in boots and cloaks, engage in a lively discussion, perhaps about the purchase of a rabbit held in the hand of the man on the far left. The legal status of the saleswoman, her assistant (?), and customers cannot be known, but their clothing, at least, suggests that all of them are ordinary folks, not the upper-class individuals in the relief from the cushion shop (see Figure 70).

The relief gives a sense of the liveliness of the Roman street and market. Customers chatted about merchandise, chickens squawked, and monkeys chattered. Tradeswomen and tradesmen displayed their wares; buyers and passersby strolled and gathered at shops and booths, drawn by the goods on display or the novelty of a couple of pet monkeys. The poet Martial, for one, adds to this picture: in the streets of

72. Relief of a butcher's shop, Rome, c. 100–150 CE. (Alinari/Art Resource, New York)

Rome, the activities of barbers, barkeepers, cooks, and butchers spill into the crowded streets, and pedestrians have to navigate around barbers shaving men in the street and barkeepers serving their customers (7.61). In this environment, the slave in a tunic perhaps blended in, joining the crowds of other ordinary Romans in simple dress – and without attendants. Unlike the workers in the cushion shop catering to upper-class customers, slaves in this situation participated more directly in the entertainments of the market and its varied social exchanges.

Two reliefs suggest the relations stemming from work, although it should be noted that these representations have been the subject of scholarly debate. A relief from Rome (mid-second century CE) depicts a butcher's shop (Figure 72). The butcher, dressed in a simple tunic, cuts ribs on a chopping block; over him hangs a rack with prepared cuts of pork, and behind him is another cleaver and a set of scales. Opposite, a woman sitting in a high-backed chair writes on tablets; she wears a long tunic and a mantle and has an elaborate hairdo. He does manual work, she records. It has been suggested that she is a bookkeeper or a scribe, working freelance or for a family member, but her relation to the butcher is curious, especially in light of her rather elegant dress and hairstyle. She does not act like customers in other reliefs and paintings. If she is a relation of the butcher or his wife, the contrast of the well-coifed writing woman and the laboring man, perhaps, reflects two sides of their lives. We might also wonder whether she might not be the owner of the butcher shop keeping track of the business side of things.

A funerary altar from Rome leads us back to the question of slaves in the city's workshops and to a scenario that appears often in the epitaphs from the city of Rome (Figure 73). The inscription on one side of the altar reads: "Lucius Cornelius Atimetus (made this) for himself and for his freedman Lucius Cornelius Epaphra and for the rest of his freedmen and freedwomen and their descendents." The relief on one side of the altar puts viewers in the workshop: two smiths (tool makers?) work together at an anvil. Between the two men is the forge with its flames, and behind the man on the left are the bellows. The seated man holds a metal object and the standing one raises a hammer to strike it. Behind them, hanging from a rod, are a pincers and various cutting tools. The other side puts viewers in the shop: two men stand beside a counter with a cabinet in which various tools are arranged by their type. Where the two smiths at work cannot be distinguished by activity or dress, in the shop, dress separates the two men – one in a toga, the dress of the Roman citizen, and the other in a tunic.

Atimetus's epitaph singles out one of his freedmen, Epaphra, by name, so we would assume that the two smiths at work are ex-master Atimetus and ex-slave Epaphra. The problem comes with the shop scene. Some scholars argue that these are the same two men, divided by dress in this scene, as they are united by work in the other. As citizens, both men (Atimetus did not note his status as a freedman or a freeborn citizen) had the right to wear the toga, so some scholars have proposed that the man in the toga is a customer, and the other in the tunic is Atimetus, gesturing toward his wares. Yet the dedication delineates Atimetus's special relation with his ex-slave, and the two sides may depict two sides of a relationship that was unequal in origin and equal in its shared labor. Perhaps if, in fact, Atimetus is the man in the toga, and Epaphra the man in the tunic, we should see the two scenes chronologically – before and after the manumission of Epaphra.

The altar's epitaph fits into a pattern found in epitaphs of artisans from the city of Rome and points to a trajectory in the lives of slave

73. Reliefs on the Funerary Altar of Atimetus, Rome, mid-first century CE. (Photo Vatican Museums)

artisans laboring in small shops like that of Atimetus and Epaphra. Among the artisans from the city of Rome identified by their occupational titles, slaves working outside the large domestic household do not appear as often as their freed counterparts, or, to put this another way, most often we glimpse slave artisans working in the market *after* they had achieved their freedom. Many, at least at death, shared a tomb with their ex-master and/or fellow freedmen like the tailors named Avilius/a, discussed in the last chapter. A marble plaque typical of those in *columbaria* more closely parallels the funerary altar of Atimetus and Epaphra, although the latter could afford a more expensive commemoration: "Marcus Sergius Eutychus, the freedman of Marcus, axle maker (made this) for himself and (his) patron, Marcus Sergius Philocalus, the freedman of Marcus, axle maker" (*Corpus of Latin Inscriptions* 6.9215, Rome). Eutychus, axle maker and freedman, dedicates an epitaph for himself and his ex-master, Philocalus, like him a freed slave and an axle maker. We should perhaps see them in a shop working together like Atimetus and Epaphra.

At this level of society, the world of small-scale artisans, slavery meant training in the trade of one's owner, where that owner was him- or herself an artisan or shopkeeper. If these epitaphs reflect social reality, the opportunities for manumission in this world of work were good, and a freed slave became what his or her ex-master was – an artisan with a shop, who often was a freed slave. Moreover, in this world, at least at death, the relations of former slaves and former owners appear familial and more equitable than the relations between Cicero and Tiro or Pliny and Encolpius, which are so eloquently articulated by the slaveholders themselves. Unlike Epaphra and Eutychus, neither Tiro nor Encolpius could step into his former owner's position.

Although these artisans belonged to the world of Roman slavery, their enslavement seems giant steps away from the slave servants in elite households and the slave laborers on country estates. Yet this gap, too, is typical of the complexity of slavery in the Roman world. The study of slave labor gives us a picture of the variety of Roman slavery. Farming, herding, baking, making and selling, serving, cleaning, and cooking – Roman slaves did it all, but they labored at these tasks in different sites and circumstances for slaveholders as grand as the politician Pliny and as ordinary as the smith Atimetus. Some slaves worked side by side with their owners: they could expect their freedom and, perhaps, their own shops. Others labored in the fields in chains or under the close supervision of foremen: they had few opportunities for eventual liberation or independence. Still other slaves waited on elite men and women, living at the margins of elegance or at their owner's side, near the rich and great but worlds away in terms of social standing, although some could hope that diligence and loyalty would have its rewards.

Such variation parallels the internal complexity of Roman slavery. Slaveholders held the power to demand of their slaves the labor that produced their own livelihoods or social standing, and thus, slave owners set the conditions of slave lives. Slave men and women, however, were not machines turned on and off with a switch: they were agents – albeit often within limited conditions for action. Some resisted; some simply managed to survive chains and whip; some found the means to better their lot – taking food and goods, setting their own pace and paths, forming friendships, communities, and families where they could. Some slaves, like the litter bearer Iucundus described at the beginning of Chapter 4, found a sense of dignity in their labor or despite it. Where the ancient sources for Roman slavery speak clearly and loudly about owners' domination, historians' careful analysis of these sources produces frequent "maybes" and "perhapses" when we talk about slaves. Yet the study of labor highlights what we have seen in other chapters – slave agency. In the epitaphs of slaves, we have a glimpse of the identities crafted by slaves, and in the slaveholders' literature and law, complaints about slaves' laziness, carelessness, theft, truancy, and flight all testify to a masterly domination limited by the actions and wills of slaves.

GLOSSARY

Terms used infrequently and defined in the text are not included here.

atriensis   Originally, the chief steward in charge of the house; later, also an ordinary house servant located in the atrium.

Augustales   Official boards of priests, usually freed slaves, whose actions honored the emperor and made various donations to their communities.

beneficium   Favor, kindness; the owner's manumission of a slave was considered a *beneficium*.

catasta   Platform on which slaves stood when they were displayed for sale.

client   Free man who, as the dependent of a wealthy man (the patron), was supposed to attend his patron's morning reception, accompany him to the forum, and, in the Republic, vote for him.

collegium   Self-help association; there were various types of *collegia*: household, occupational, burial.

collibertus, -a   Fellow ex-slave.

columbarium   Chamber tomb whose walls were lined with niches for ash urns and accompanying plaques.

Compitalia   Festival of the Crossroads, celebrated in Rome and the countryside in late December/early January.

conservus, -a   Fellow slave.

consul   Highest office in the Roman state, which enobled its holders and their descendants.

contubernalis   Tent mate, housemate, close friend, or slave's spouse.

cubicularius   Bedchamber servant.

delicia   Favorites, pets; slave children who were their owners' favorites.

denarius   Most common silver coin from the late third century BCE to the third century CE.

dispensator   Administrator concerned with finances; steward.

Edict of the Aediles   Edict of the magistrates who supervised the markets; it laid out the rules governing the sale of slaves.

empire, Empire   Empire (with a lowercase e) refers to the provinces and areas ruled by Rome; Empire (with an uppercase E) refers to the Principate, the period when Rome and the empire were ruled by an emperor.

equestrians   Wealthy individuals belonging to a privileged group who had the highest rating in the census; generally, they did not run for office and enter the senate.

ergastulum   Slave prison.

familia   Slaves of a single owner or household.

familia rustica   Slaves working on a farm.

familia urbana   Slaves working in an urban household.

genius   Spirit of an individual, place, or activity.

iniuria   Injury or insult; the law on *iniuria* protected the physical integrity and honor of freeborn citizens.

iugerum   Roman measurement of land, approximately two-thirds of an acre.

lararium   Shrine for *lares*.

lares   Protecting spirits; *lares familiares* were family and household gods.

lecticarius   Litter bearer.

libertinus, -a; libertus, -a   In relation to society, an ex-slave was called a *libertinus/-a*; in relation to his or her former owner, a *libertus/-a*.

manumission   Freeing of a slave.

medicus, -a   Doctor; perhaps the female *medica* was a midwife.

modius   A unit of dry measure equal to 8.7 liters.

natio   Origin, people.

nobles   Men who had attained the consulship or their descendents; nobles were the most privileged and prestigious group in Roman society.

obsequium   Proper respect, which in the case of freed slaves, meant compliance and accommodation to the will of their former owners.

operae   Workdays often required of freed slaves for which a sum of money could be substituted.

paedagogium   Training establishment for a household's slaves, which often included their living space.

palla   Mantle worn by women as an outdoor garment.

paterfamilias   Male head of the family (usually a father) who had power over the family members and slaves in his *potestas*.

patria potestas   The power and authority of a *paterfamilias*.

patron   In regard to a freed slave, the term means ex-master; in regard to a client, an individual of higher standing and wealth who was supposed to provide his client with food, assistance, and protection.

peculium   "Purse," the property controlled by a son in *potestas* or a slave, which legally belonged to the father or owner.

plebs   Ordinary Romans, the common people.

princeps   Roman term for emperor.

Principate   Period after 27 BCE when Rome and its empire was ruled by an emperor (the *princeps*).

publicani   Equestrian tax collectors.

quadrantal   Roman liquid measure equal to about 6 gallons.

quaestor   First office on the Roman hierarchy of magistracies; quaestors had financial responsibilities.

Republic   Period from 509 to 27 BCE when Rome was ruled by an oligarchy of senators and nobles.

Saturnalia   Holiday celebrated in late December by public sacrifices and private feasts in the household; the festival included gift giving and the exchange of roles by slaves and owners.

senate   Chief body of the Roman state filled with ex-magistrates.

senators   Members of the senate; the senatorial order was a social and political elite.

servus, -a   Slave.

sestertius   Originally a silver coin, but from Augustus on minted in bronze; equivalent to one-fourth of a denarius; English plural, sesterces.

Stoicism   Greek philosophical movement adopted and adapted by upper-class Romans that emphasized virtue and reason.

stola   Long outer garment worn only by proper Roman citizen women.

sui iuris   Independent; the condition of a freeborn Roman citizen whose *paterfamilias* had died.

supra lecticarios   Supervisor of litter bearers.

Tiro   Secretary and freedman of Cicero.

Trimalchio   Fictional wealthy, vulgar ex-slave featured in an episode of Petronius's novel the *Satyricon*.

verna   Home-born slave; a slave born in a Roman household rather than a captive or a slave purchased in the marketplace.

vicarius, -a   Slave of a slave.

vilica   Wife of the *vilicus* who had her own supervisory duties.

vilicus   Manager or overseer (usually a slave) of a farm and its slave workers.

villa rustica   Farmhouse.

villa urbana   City house; country residence of wealthy owner.

virtus   Manly courage, achieved primarily in battle.

ANCIENT SOURCES

Slaves and slavery appear in a wide variety of sources from the Roman world. The following list includes only those mentioned in this book. Many of them are available in English translations from the Loeb Classical Library (abbreviated *LCL* in the main text), Penguin Books, and World Classics (Oxford University Press). Two collections of sources, translated into English are especially useful:

Wiedemann, T. E. J. 1981. *Greek and Roman Slavery*. London: Routledge.

Gardner, J. F., and T. E. J. Wiedemann. 1991. *The Roman Household: A Sourcebook*. London: Routledge.

Appian (active second century CE)   Born in Alexandria, he became a Roman citizen and moved to Rome. His history of Rome, written in Greek, is organized by the peoples conquered by the Romans and includes several books on the civil struggles of the late second and first centuries BCE.

Apuleius (c. 125–170 CE)   Born in north Africa, he wrote a novel, *Metamorphoses* (or *The Golden Ass*), in which the narrator is turned into an ass by magic and journeys all over Greece from adventure to adventure.

Gaius Julius Caesar (100–44 BCE)   Famous as a politician, the conqueror of Gaul, and, finally as dictator, his assassination sparked the struggle that ended in the foundation of the Principate. He wrote accounts of his campaigns in Gaul and in the civil war of the early 40s BCE.

Cato the Elder (234–149 BCE) Orator, politician, and author, he was famous as a moralist (censor in 184 BCE). He wrote the earliest extant agricultural handbook in Latin, *On Agriculture.*

Cicero (106–43 BCE) Famous as a politician and orator, he wrote many speeches, letters, and philosophical works.

Columella (active mid-first century CE) Author of the longest, most systematic, and most detailed agricultural handbook, *On Agriculture.*

Corpus of Latin Inscriptions The *Corpus Inscriptionum Latinarum* is the largest collections of Latin inscriptions; it includes inscriptions from all over the Roman empire.

Digest This compilation of Roman law was put together in the early sixth century CE under the emperor Justinian; it preserves earlier laws, edicts, and imperial orders. For an English translation, see A. Watson, ed. and trans., *The Digest of Justinian* (Philadelphia: University of Pennsylvania Press, 1985).

Diodorus Siculus (active first century BCE) Born in Sicily, he wrote a world history from its mythological origins to 60 BCE. He focuses on Greece and Sicily.

Dionysius of Halicarnassus (active late first century BCE) Greek historian and rhetorician, he came to Rome under Augustus. He wrote critical works and *Roman Antiquities* (a history of Rome to 246 BCE).

Festus (active late second century CE) A scholar, he abridged *On the Meaning of Words* by Verrius Flaccus, a scholar and antiquarian active under Augustus.

Florentinus (active second century CE) Author of an introductory work on law, the *Institutes.*

Gaius (active second century CE) A teacher of law, he wrote extensively; his *Institutes* was a textbook for beginners in the study of Roman law. For an English translation, see F. de Zulueta, ed. and trans., *The Institutes of Gaius,* 2 vols. (Oxford: Clarendon Press, 1969).

Galen (c. 129?–199/216 CE)   From Pergamum in Asia Minor, he began his career as a doctor for gladiators and rose to the position of physician in the court of Marcus Aurelius. He wrote philosophical as well as medical works.

Horace (65–8 BCE)   Poet in the Rome of Augustus, he wrote poetic letters, lyric poetry, and satires.

Juvenal (active late first–early second centuries CE)   His satires attack a wide range of figures in Roman society: the wealthy, pretentious foreigners and freedmen, decadent nobles, and women.

Labeo (active late first century BCE–early first century CE)   An influential teacher of law, he wrote over 400 books, none of which survive; we know about his work through versions abbreviated by later jurists.

Livy (59 BCE–17 CE)   He wrote a history of Rome from its foundation to 9 BCE.

Martial (c. 38/41–104 CE)   He wrote epigrams, short poems on events, people, and the conditions of Roman society.

Petronius (active mid-first century CE)   Senator and consul, he was probably the famous arbiter of elegance in the court of Nero. His novel the *Satyricon* traces the adventures of a hero and his friends. One of its episodes describes the fabulously wealthy ex-slave Trimalchio.

Phaedrus (c. 15 BCE–c. 50 CE)   A slave freed by the emperor Augustus, he is the author of a five-book work of verse fables, many of which, he claims, were based on the fables of Aesop.

Plautus (active late third–early second centuries BCE)   The plays of this popular comic poet feature a variety of slave characters and their owners.

Pliny the Elder (c. 23–79 CE)   He held important equestrian posts in the army under Vespasian and Titus and commanded the fleet at Misenum when Vesuvius erupted in 79 CE. He wrote an encyclopedia, *The Natural History,* which covers the natural world, geography, art, and medicine.

Pliny the Younger (61/2–113 CE)   The nephew and adopted son of Pliny the Elder, he was a famous orator, politician, and imperial governor; he published an oration praising the emperor Trajan and ten books of his letters.

Plutarch (before 50–after 120 CE) Resident of Charonea, this Greek author wrote paired biographies of famous Greeks and Romans, antiquarian works, and philosophical tracts.

Polybius (c. 200–c. 118 BCE) An important figure in the Achaean League in Greece, he was one of 1,000 important Achaeans deported to Rome after 167 BCE. He became a friend and companion of the important Roman politician and general Scipio Aemilianus; his *Histories* trace Rome's rise to power in the Mediterranean in the third–second centuries BCE.

Select Latin Inscriptions *Inscriptiones Latinae Selectae* is a large collection of inscriptions, edited by H. Dessau.

Seneca (4 BCE/1 CE–65 CE) A famous orator and politician, he was the tutor of the young emperor Nero; he wrote many philosophical works.

Tacitus (c. 56–120 CE) A senator and famous orator, he wrote histories of imperial Rome: the *Annals* covering the reigns of Tiberius through Nero and the *Histories* covering the civil war of 68–69 and the Flavian emperors.

Twelve Tables (451/450 BCE) The earliest written Roman law, these ordinances are known from passages in later authors.

Ulpian (active early third century CE) Member of the imperial council and praetorian prefect under the emperor Alexander Severus (222–235 CE), he wrote a lengthy commentary on the Praetor's Edict.

Valerius Maximus (active early first century CE) Author of a collection of illustrative examples of virtues and vices, he recounts many short stories and historical episodes.

Varro (116–27 BCE) A renowned scholar and antiquarian, he wrote on a wide variety of topics. His work *On Agriculture* covers different forms of farming and stock raising.

SELECT BIBLIOGRAPHY

The bibliography on Roman slavery is huge; the works listed below (including other works referred to in the main text) represent only a small proportion of the scholarly work in English. Readers should be aware that the study of Roman slavery is an international endeavor of conferences and publications sponsored by institutes devoted to the study of ancient slavery: in England, the Institute for the Study of Slavery (ISOS); in France, the Groupe Internationale de Researche sur l'Esclavage dans l'Antiquité (International Group for the Research on Ancient Slavery [GIREA]); and in Germany, Forschungen zur antiken Sklaverei (Researches on Ancient Slavery).

Beard, M. (2002). "Ciceronian Correspondences: Making a Book Out of Letters." In T. P. Wiseman, ed., *Classics in Progress: Essays on Ancient Greece and Rome,* 103–144. Oxford: Oxford University Press.

Bodel, J. (2005). "*Caveat Emptor*: Towards a Study of Roman Slave-traders." *Journal of Roman Archaeology* 18: 181–195.

Bradley, K. R. (1978). "Holidays for Slaves." *Symbolae Osloenses* 54: 111–118.

(1986). "Seneca and Slavery." *Classica et Mediaevalia* 37: 161–172.

(1987a). "On the Roman Slave Supply and Slave-breeding." In M. I. Finley, ed., *Classical Slavery,* 43–64. London: Frank Cass.

(1987b). *Slaves and Masters in the Roman Empire.* Oxford: Oxford University Press.

(1989). *Slavery and Rebellion in the Roman World 140–70 BC.* Bloomington: Indiana University Press.

(1990). "*Servus Onerosus*: Roman Law and the Troublesome Slave." *Slavery and Abolition* 11: 135–157.

(1992). "'The Regular, Daily Traffic in Slaves': Roman History and Contemporary History." *Classical Journal* 87: 125–138.

(1994). *Slavery and Society at Rome.* Cambridge: Cambridge University Press.

(2000). "Animalizing the Slave: The Truth of Fiction." *Journal of Roman Studies* 90: 110–125.

(2004). "On Captives under the Principate." *Phoenix* 58: 298–318.

Bradley, M. (2002). "'It all comes out in the wash': Looking Harder at the Roman Fullonica." *Journal of Roman Archaeology* 15: 20–44.

Brunt, P. A. (1987 [1971]). *Italian Manpower 225 B.C.–A.D. 14.* Oxford: Clarendon Press.

(1980). "Free Labour and Public Works." *Journal of Roman Studies* 70: 81–100.

Buckland, W. W. (1970 [1908]). *The Roman Law of Slavery.* Cambridge: Cambridge University Press.

Butler, S. (1998). "Notes on a *Membrum Disiectum*." In S. R. Joshel and S. Murnaghan, eds., *Women and Slaves in Greco-Roman Culture: Differential Equations,* 236–255. New York: Routledge.

Camp, S. M. H. (2004). *Closer to Freedom: Enslaved Women and Everyday Resistance in the Plantation South.* Chapel Hill: University of North Carolina Press.

Clark, J. R. (2003). *Art in the Lives of Ordinary Romans.* Berkeley: University of California Press.

Clark, P. (1998). "Women, Slaves and the Hierarchies of Domestic Violence: The Family of St. Augustine." In S. R, Joshel and S. Murnaghan, eds., *Women and Slaves in Greco-Roman Culture: Differential Equations,* 109–129. New York and London: Routledge.

Combes, I. A. H. (1998). *The Metaphor of Slavery in the Writings of the Early Church: From the New Testament to the Beginnings of the Fifth Century.* Sheffield: Sheffield Academic Press.

Cornell, T. J. (1995). *The Beginnings of Rome: Italy and Rome from the Bronze Age to the Punic Wars (c. 1000–264 BC)*. London: Routledge.

Crook, J. A. (1967). *Law and Life of Rome*. London: Thames and Hudson.

D'Arms, J. H. (1981). *Commerce and Social Standing in Ancient Rome*. Cambridge, MA: Harvard University Press.

(1991). "Slaves at the Roman *Convivia*." In W. J. Slater, ed., *Dining in a Classical Context*, 171–183. Ann Arbor: University of Michigan Press.

Davis, D. B. (2001). *In the Image of God: Religion, Moral Values, and Our Heritage of Slavery*. New Haven, CT: Yale University Press.

Douglass, F. (1962 [1892]). *Life and Times of Frederick Douglass Written by Himself*. New York: Macmillan.

Duff, A. M. (1928). *Freedmen in the Roman Empire*. Oxford: Clarendon Press.

Dunbabin, K. M. D. (2003). *The Roman Banquet: Images of Conviviality*. Cambridge: Cambridge University Press.

Duncan-Jones, R. (1982 [1974]). *The Economy of the Roman Empire: Quantitative Studies*. Cambridge: Cambridge University Press.

Finley, M. I. (1980). *Ancient Slavery and Modern Ideology*. New York: Viking.

Fitzgerald, W. (2000). *Slavery and the Roman Literary Imagination*. Cambridge: Cambridge University Press.

Fleming, R. (1999). "*Quae Corpore Quaestum Facit*: The Sexual Economy of Female Prostitution in the Roman Empire." *Journal of Roman Studies* 89: 38–61.

Flory, M. B. (1978). "Family in *Familia*: Kinship and Community in Slavery." *American Journal of Ancient History* 3(1): 78–95.

Forbes, C. A. (1955). "The Education and Training of Slaves in Antiquity." *Transactions of the American Philological Association* 86: 321–360.

Gardner, J. F. (1993). *Being a Roman Citizen*. New York: Routledge.

(1998). *Family and Familia in Roman Law and Life*. Oxford: Clarendon Press.

Garnsey, P. (1968). "Legal Privilege in the Roman Empire." *Past and Present* 41: 3–24.

(1970). *Social Status and Legal Privilege in the Roman Empire.* Oxford: Clarendon Press.

(1980). "Non-slave Labour in the Roman World." In P. Garnsey, ed., *Non-slave Labour in Graeco-Roman Antiquity. Proceedings of the Cambridge Philological Society,* suppl. vol. 6, 4–47. Cambridge.

(1981). "Independent Freedmen and the Economy of Roman Italy under the Principate." *Klio* 63: 359–371.

(1996). *Ideas of Slavery from Aristotle to Augustine.* Cambridge: Cambridge University Press.

George, M. (1997a). "Repopulating the Roman House." In B. Rawson and P. R. C. Weaver, eds., *The Roman Family in Italy,* 299–319. Oxford: Clarendon Press.

(1997b). "*Servus* and *Domus:* The Slave in the Roman House." In R. Laurence and A. Wallace-Hadrill, eds., *Domestic Space in the Roman World. Journal of Roman Archaeology* suppl. 22, 15–24. Portsmouth.

Graham, E.-J. (2006). *The Burial of the Urban Poor in Italy in the Late Roman Republic and Early Empire. British Archaeological Reports, International Series* 1565. Oxford.

Harris, W. V. (1979). *War and Imperialism in Republican Rome 327–70 BC.* Oxford: Clarendon Press.

(1980). "A Study of the Roman Slave Trade." In J. H. D'Arms and E. C. Kopff, eds., *The Seaborne Commerce of Ancient Rome, Memoirs of the American Academy in Rome* 36, 117–140. Rome.

(1994). "Child-exposure in the Roman Empire." *Journal of Roman Studies* 84: 1–22.

(1999). "Demography, Geography, and the Sources of Roman Slaves." *Journal of Roman Studies* 89: 62–75.

Hasegawa, K. (2005). *The* Familia Urbana *during the Early Empire: A Study of the* Columbaria *Inscriptions. British Archaeological Reports, International Series* 1440. Oxford.

Hopkins, K. (1978). *Conquerors and Slaves.* Cambridge: Cambridge University Press.

(1983). *Death and Renewal.* Cambridge: Cambridge University Press.

Johnson, W. (1999). *Soul by Soul: Life inside the Antebellum Slave Market.* Cambridge, MA: Harvard University Press.

Jones, C. P. (1987). "Stigma: Tattooing and Branding in Graeco-Roman Antiquity." *Journal Roman Studies* 77: 139–155.

Jongman, W. (2003). "Slavery and the Growth of Rome: The Transformation of Italy in the Second and First Centuries BCE." In C. Edwards and G. Woolf, eds., *Rome the Cosmopolis,* 100–122. Cambridge: Cambridge University Press.

Joshel, S. R. (1992). *Work, Identity and Legal Status at Rome.* Norman: University of Oklahoma Press.

Kampen, N. (1981). *Image and Status: Roman Working Women in Ostia.* Berlin: Mann.

Kleiner, D. E. E. (1977). *Roman Group Portraiture: The Funerary Reliefs of the Late Republic and Early Empire.* New York: Garland.

Loane, H. J. (1938). *Industry and Commerce of the City of Rome (50 B.C.–200 A.D.).* Baltimore: Johns Hopkins University Press.

MacMullen, R. (1974). *Roman Social Relations.* New Haven, CT: Yale University Press.

Manning, C. (1989). "Stoicism and Slavery in the Roman Empire." *Aufstieg und Niedergang der Römischen Welt* II:36.3: 1518–1563.

Martin, D. A. (1990). *Slavery as Salvation: The Metaphor of Slavery in Pauline Christianity.* New Haven, CT: Yale University Press.

McCarthy, K. (2000). *Slaves, Masters and the Art of Authority in Plautine Comedy.* Princeton, NJ: Princeton University Press.

McGinn, T. A. J. (2004). *The Economy of Prostitution in the Roman World.* Ann Arbor: University of Michigan Press.

McKeown, N. (2007). *The Invention of Ancient Slavery.* London: Duckworth.

Mirkovic, M. (1997). *The Later Roman Colonate and Freedom.* Philadelphia: American Philosophical Society.

Mohler, S. L. (1940). "Slave Education in the Roman Empire." *Transactions of the American Philological Association* 71: 262–280.

Morley, N. (1996). *Metropolis and Hinterland: The City of Rome and the Italian Economy.* Cambridge: Cambridge University Press.

(2001). "The Transformation of Italy, 225–28 B.C." *Journal of Roman Studies* 91: 50–62.

Parker, H. (1989). "Crucially Funny or Tranio on the Couch: The *Servus Callidus* and Jokes about Torture." *Transactions of the American Philological Association* 119: 233–246.

(1998). "Loyal Slaves and Loyal Wives: The Crisis of the Outsider-within and Roman *Exemplum* Literature." In S. R. Joshel and B. Murnaghan, eds., *Women and Slaves in Greco-Roman Culture: Differential Equations,* 152–173. New York: Routledge.

Parkin, T. (1992). *Demography and Roman Society.* Baltimore: Johns Hopkins University Press.

Patterson, O. (1982). *Slavery and Social Death: A Comparative Study.* Cambridge, MA: Harvard University Press.

Petersen, L. H. (2006). *The Freedman in Roman Art and Art History.* Cambridge: Cambridge University Press.

Rawson, B. (1966). "Family Life among the Lower Classes at Rome in the First Two Centuries of the Empire." *Classical Philology* 61: 71–83.

Rawson, B., ed. (1986). *The Family in Ancient Rome.* Ithaca: Cornell University Press.

Richlin, A. (1992). *The Garden of Priapus: Sexuality and Aggression in Roman Sexual Humor.* Oxford: Oxford University Press.

(2005). *Rome and the Mysterious Orient: Three Plays by Plautus.* Berkeley: University of California Press.

Roller, M. (2001). *Constructing Autocracy: Aristocrats and Emperors in Julio-Claudian Rome.* Princeton, NJ: Princeton University Press.

Roth, U. (2007). *Thinking Tools: Agricultural Slavery between Evidence and Models.* London: Bulletin of the Institute of Classical Studies.

Saller, R. (1987). "Slavery and the Roman Family." In M. I. Finley, ed., *Classical Slavery,* 65–87. London: Frank Cass.

(1994). *Patriarchy, Property and Death in the Roman Family.* Cambridge: Cambridge University Press.

(1998). "Symbols of Gender and Status Hierarchies in the Roman Household." In S. R. Joshel and B. Murnaghan, eds., *Women and Slaves in Greco-Roman Culture: Differential Equations,* 85–91. New York: Routledge.

Saller, R. P., and B. Shaw. (1984). "Tombstones and Family Relations in the Principate: Civilians, Soldiers and Slaves." *Journal of Roman Studies* 74: 124–156.

Scheidel, W. (1996). *Measuring Sex, Age and Death in the Roman Empire: Explorations in Ancient Demography. Journal of Roman Archaeology,* Supplement Volume 21. Ann Arbor, MI.

(1997). "Quantifying the Sources of Slaves in the Early Roman Empire." *Journal of Roman Studies* 87: 156–169.

(2000). "Slaves of the Soil." *Journal of Roman Archaeology* 13: 727–732.

(2004). "Human Mobility in Roman Italy, I: The Slave Population." *Journal of Roman Studies* 94: 1–26.

(2005). "Human Mobility in Roman Italy, II: The Free Population." *Journal of Roman Studies* 95: 64–79.

Shaw, B. D., ed. (1998). "'A Wolf by the Ears': M. I. Finley's Ancient Slavery and Modern Ideology in Historical Context." In M. I. Finley, *Ancient Slavery and Modern Ideology,* 3–53. Princeton, NJ: Markus Wiener.

Shaw, B. D. (2001). *Spartacus and the Slave Wars: A Brief History with Documents.* Boston: Bedford/St. Martin's.

Thalmann, W. (1997). "Versions of Slavery in the *Captivi* of Plautus." *Ramus* 25(2): 112–145.

Thompson, F. H. (2003). *The Archaeology of Greek and Roman Slavery.* London: Duckworth.

Treggiari, S. (1969). *Roman Freedmen during the Late Republic.* Oxford: Oxford University Press.

(1973). "Domestic Staff at Rome in the Julio-Claudian Period, 27 B. C. to A. D. 68." *Histoire sociale/Social history* 6(12): 241–255.

(1975a). "Family Life among the Staff of the Volusii." *Transactions of the American Philological Association* 105: 393–401.

(1975b). "Jobs in the Household of Livia." *Papers of the British School at Rome* 43: 48–77.

(1976). "Jobs for Women." *American Journal of Ancient History* 1: 76–104.

(1981). "*Contubernales* in *CIL* 6." *Phoenix* 35: 42–69.

Urbainczyk, T. (2004). *Spartacus*. London: Duckworth.

(2008). *Slave Revolts in Antiquity*. Berkeley: University of California Press.

Vogt, J. (1975). *Ancient Slavery and the Ideal of Man*. Cambridge, MA: Harvard University Press.

Wallace-Hadrill, A. (1994). *Houses and Society in Pompeii and Herculaneum*. Princeton, NJ: Princeton University Press.

Watson, A. (1987). *Roman Slave Law*. Baltimore: Johns Hopkins University Press.

Weaver, P. R. C. (1972). *Familia Caesaris: A Social Study of the Emperor's Freedmen and Slaves*. Cambridge: Cambridge University Press.

Westermann, W. L. (1955). *The Slave Systems of Greek and Roman Antiquity*. Memoirs of the American Philosophical Society, vol. 40. Philadelphia.

Whittaker, C. R. (1987). "Circe's Pigs: From Slavery to Serfdom in the Late Roman World." In M. I. Finley, ed., *Classical Slavery*, 88–122. London: Frank Cass.

Wiedemann, T. E. J. (1985). "The Regularity of Manumission at Rome." *Classical Quarterly* 35: 162–175.

Wirszubski, C. (1960). *Libertas as a Political Idea at Rome during the Late Republic and Early Principate*. Cambridge: Cambridge University Press.

INDEX